HOLIDAY FUN

To: Roma, Ralph & Jody

From: Mom & Dad.

To help you to keep Jody Busy

June 2007.

KINGFISHER
Larousse Kingfisher Chambers Inc.
95 Madison Avenue
New York, New York 10016

First published in 2000
The material in this edition was previously published in six individual volumes
in 1993, 1994, 1995, and 1996

2 4 6 8 10 9 7 5 3 1

1TR / 0300 /EDK / HBM (UNV) / 100WF

LIBRARY OF CONGRESS CATALOGING-IN-PUBLICATION DATA
has been applied for.

ISBN 0-7534-5314-2

Authors: Judy Bastyra (*Hanukkah Fun*), Ronne Randall (*Thanksgiving Fun*), Linda Robertson
(*Kwanzaa Fun*), Deri Robins (*Easter Fun* and *Christmas Fun*), Abigail Willis (*Halloween Fun*)

Illustrators: Maggie Downer (*Easter Fun* and *Christmas Fun*), Julia Pearson (*Kwanzaa Fun*),
Annabel Spenceley (*Halloween Fun* and *Thanksgiving Fun*), Catherine Ward (*Hanukkah Fun*)

Printed in Spain

HOLIDAY FUN

NEW YORK

CONTENTS

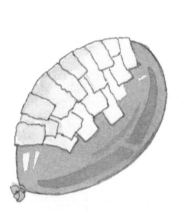

CHRISTMAS FUN

KWANZAA FUN

EASTER FUN

EASTER TIME

The long, dark winter months are over—spring has finally arrived! There are signs of new life everywhere—leaves and buds cover the trees, birds start building their nests, and each day is a little longer than the one before it.

People have celebrated the arrival of spring for thousands of years. Long ago, winter meant great hardship for most people. Their homes were dark and cold, and food supplies often ran dangerously low. When spring came around again and new crops began to grow, it was a time of great rejoicing. The people gave thanks to the goddess Eostre, from whose name we get our word "Easter."

Today, many religious festivals are held in the spring. There's Easter itself, of course—one of the most important dates in the Christian calendar. The Jewish Passover and the Indian festival of Holi are also held at this time. For everyone, it's a time for fun, celebration, and new beginnings.

There's plenty to do, so let's get going!

SEEDS FOR SPRING

Everywhere you look, trees and flowers are putting out shoots and leaves. You can make a springtime garden on your own windowsill—all you need are some seeds!

You will need

Apples, oranges, lemons, and grapes (All have seeds inside from which new plants can grow. Use them to grow pretty houseplants—they may even bear fruit one day, but don't count on it!)

1 Fill a small seed tray with potting soil (or use a clean plastic container). Bury some seeds in the soil, about 3" apart.

3 When the shoots have about four leaves, plant them in separate flower-pots.

You can also try planting garlic cloves, or the top of an onion.

2 Water the soil, and put the tray in a warm, light place until shoots start to appear.

orange plant

onion plant

PAPER FLOWERS

If you can't wait for the springtime flowers to come out, you can make a bright bouquet of paper blooms—they'll come in handy for decorating your Easter bonnet, and would also make a great gift for Mother's Day!

You will need

crepe paper in different colors (including green)
green paper, thin cardboard
thin garden wire, or some thin sticks
cotton balls
scissors, glue

1 Ask an adult to cut a piece of wire about 10" long (or use a thin stick). Tape a cotton ball to one end of the wire or stick.

2 Cut a small square of crepe paper and tie over the cotton ball.

3 Cut a long strip of the same paper, about 2½" wide. Fold it over about eight times to make a zigzag.

4 Draw one of these petal shapes onto the strip of paper and cut out to make eight petals.

5 Glue each petal just below the cotton ball wad, overlapping them slightly.

6 Cut a long, thin strip of green crepe paper. Glue one end around the top of the stem, wind tightly down like a bandage, and glue the other end to the bottom.

7 Cut more leaves out of cardboard, and glue these along the stem. When dry, gently pull back the edges of the petals.

This daffodil has a center made of paper, which is glued in separately.

Try cutting the petals into tiny strips to make a carnation.

CARDS FOR EASTER

Bunnies, chicks, and spring flowers all make good subjects for Easter cards—take your pick! The window box would also make a great Mother's Day card....

You will need

thin cardboard (15"x6")
scissors, glue
white tissue paper
scraps of fabric
colored construction
paper

WINDOW BOX

1 Fold the cardboard into thirds. Cut a window out of *a*. Fold over, draw an identical window onto *b*, and cut this out.

2 Glue tissue paper over window *b*. Stick a piece of fabric down on top, to make a shade. Then glue *a* on top of *b*.

3 Cut a window box out of cardboard and glue to the front. Cut flowers, leaves, and stems out of construction paper, and glue these on, too.

ZIGZAG CHICKS

You will need

colored construction paper
a pencil
scissors
glue

1 Cut a strip of cardboard about 12"x4". Fold it into a zigzag as shown.

2 Copy this chick shape onto the zigzag, keeping the two folded edges on the left.

3 Cut out the animal shape. Make sure you don't cut through the parts that touch the folded edges. Open out the zigzag.

4 Decorate one side of the zigzag by cutting shapes out of colored paper and gluing them down.

You can make Easter bunnies in the same way!

ALL ABOUT EGGS

Easter wouldn't be Easter without eggs! All around the world, children look forward to a visit from the Easter Bunny, who hides eggs around the house and yard. There are all kinds of eggy games to play, too—like tossing hard-boiled eggs in the air, racing with an egg on a spoon, or rolling them down a hill! Decorating eggs is another important tradition. Here are some ideas to try.

BLOWING EGGS

Blown eggs are more fragile than hard-boiled ones, but you can pack them away after Easter and keep them for many years to come.

Make a hole in each end with a pin. Then carefully make the holes bigger with a nail (the bottom hole needs to be about $1/2''$ across, but the top can be much smaller).

Hold the egg over a bowl, and blow out the yolk and white. Keep these for cooking. The egg is easier to decorate if you push a knitting needle through the holes. Hold in place with modeling clay.

14

COLORED EGGS

You will need

eggs (white ones are best for dyeing)
food for making dyes—try onion skins, raw beets, turmeric, spinach leaves, or grapes
vinegar

1 Half fill a small saucepan with water. Add drops of vinegar and one of the following: onion or spinach leaves, half a beet, a heaped teaspoon of turmeric, or a few grapes.

2 Ask an adult to boil the water for 30 minutes. Dip eggs in the water when it has cooled, and leave until they change color. Leave to dry.

PRETTY PATTERNS

You will need

masking tape
food dyes or paint

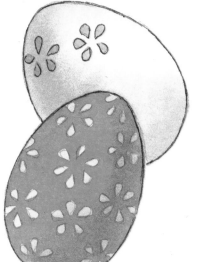

1 Cut the masking tape into shapes—like the petals of a flower. Press gently but firmly onto the egg.

2 Dye the egg or paint all over the shell. When dry, peel off the masking tape to see the pattern.

EGGCELLENT IDEAS

You can simply paint the eggs freehand or glue on paper flowers, lace, and braid. Try turning the eggs into faces or animals. Cloth, paper, and yarn make hair, tails, and ears.

1 Cut a potato in half and cut a simple pattern on the flat surface. Dip into paint and press *gently* onto the surface of the egg, to make a repeating pattern.

2 Wash your egg out carefully, and ask an adult to help you fill it with melted chocolate or Jell-O. Put it in the fridge to set—and give someone a surprise at breakfast!

16

PAPIER MÂCHÉ EGGS

You will need

an oval balloon
newspaper
2 cups flour
4 cups water
paints
varnish

1 Ask an adult to heat the water and flour in a pan until the mixture looks like cake batter. Let it cool.

2 Tear the paper into small strips. Ask an adult to blow up the balloon.

3 Dip the paper strips into the paste, and smooth them onto the balloon. Make at least seven layers.

Finish off with a coat of varnish.

4 When it's dry paint it to look like a big Easter egg, or cut it in half into two Mardi Gras masks!

BOXES AND BASKETS

Jelly beans and Easter eggs look even more exciting when they come in a special basket—here's how to make your own out of paper.

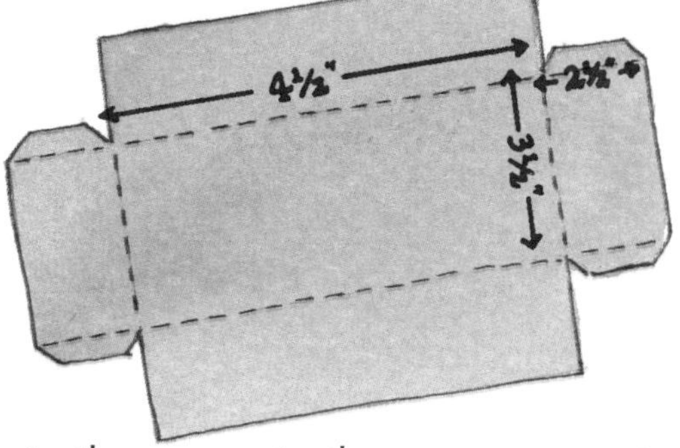

4½" 2½" 3½"

BUNNY BASKET

All you need is some colored construction paper a pencil and ruler scissors and glue

1 Copy the above pattern onto the paper, to the measurements given. Cut out and fold up to make a box. Then glue the flaps inside the box as shown below.

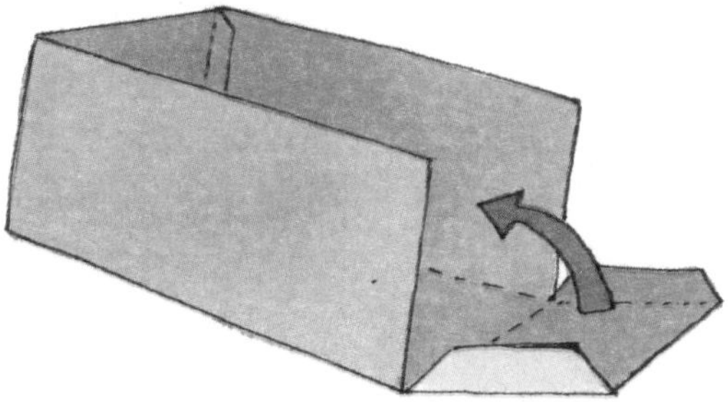

2 Fold a piece of paper in half and then draw a long-eared bunny's head on the front. Cut out the shape, but *don't* cut the top of the ears.

3 Glue the bunny to the basket—the ears will make the handles. Line with crumpled tissue paper.

WOVEN BASKETS

Again, all you will need is some colored construction paper
a pencil and ruler
scissors, and
glue

½"
border

1 Copy this pattern onto the paper, to the given measurements. Cut it out.

3½"
3½"
3½"

2 Cut six slits on each side. Leave a border about ½" wide along the top of each side.

3 Cut six strips of colored paper, each about ½"x 12" long.

4 Fold up the sides of the box. Weave a strip through all four sides, as shown. Glue the ends down.

5 Continue weaving up to the top. Go *over* the slits where the strip below went *under*. Glue on a handle and add decorations.

19

FUNNY BUNNY

Cute fluffy bunnies (not to mention chicks and lambs) can easily be made from yarn pompoms!

You will need

cardboard
scissors
thick yarn
scraps of felt
pipe cleaners

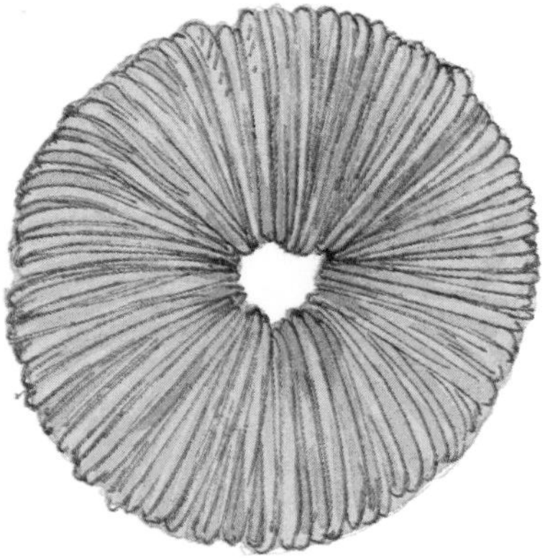

1 Wind some yarn around two rings cut out of cardboard (3″ across).

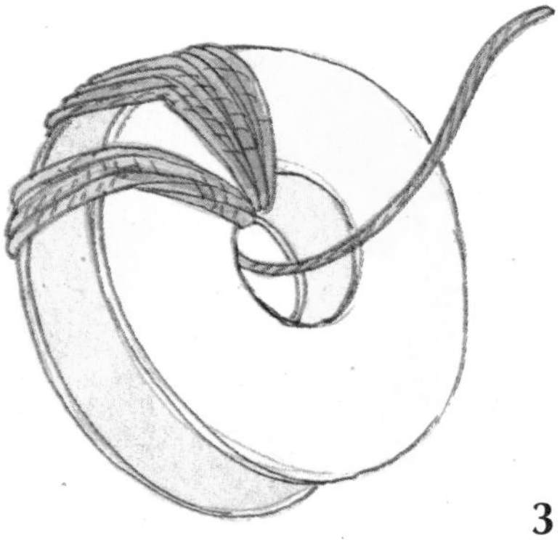

2 Keep winding pieces of yarn around the rings, until the hole in the middle is nearly full.

3 Ask an adult to push the point of the scissors between the rings, and cut the yarn.

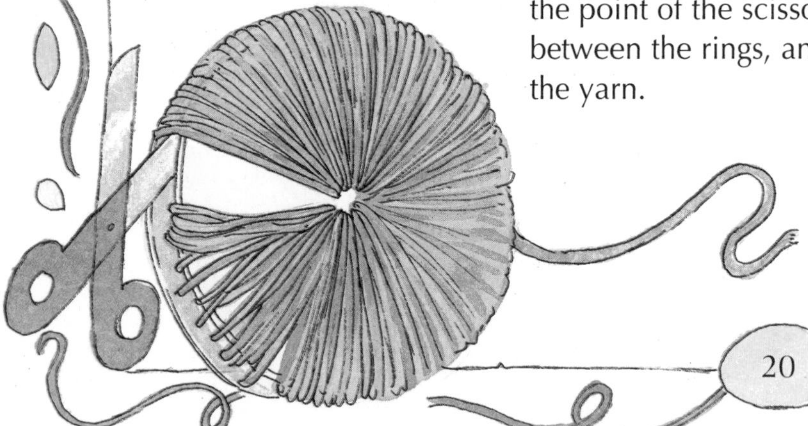

4 Ease the rings slightly apart, and tie a piece of yarn firmly around the middle. Pull off the rings.

5 Make another pompom, using rings about 1$\frac{1}{2}$″ wide. Tie the pompoms together with the loose pieces of yarn.

▲ A brown or gray Easter bunny can have a pair of floppy felt ears and a felt nose. Sew on small beads or buttons for eyes.

▶ Sew or glue a diamond of felt to this chick's head. To make legs, just wind a pipe cleaner around the middle of the body before tying on the head.

◀ Make a lamb from white pompoms, add floppy black felt ears and a tail, and two pipe cleaners for legs.

Think up some more baby animals to add to your spring collection!

21

EASTER BONNETS

To make a hat or bonnet for the Easter parade, you'll need thin cardboard, colored construction paper, paints, glue, and scissors. For the bonnet, you'll also need paper flowers (pages 10-11).

FLOWER BONNETS

1 Cut a circle out of cardboard, following this pattern. Cut it out and paint it to look like a straw bonnet.

2 Draw a little circle in the center and draw four lines inside it. Cut along these lines. Bend up as shown.

3 Make lots of paper flowers (see page 10-11), keeping the stems short.

4 Glue the flowers all around the brim of the hat, overlapping them to hide the stems.

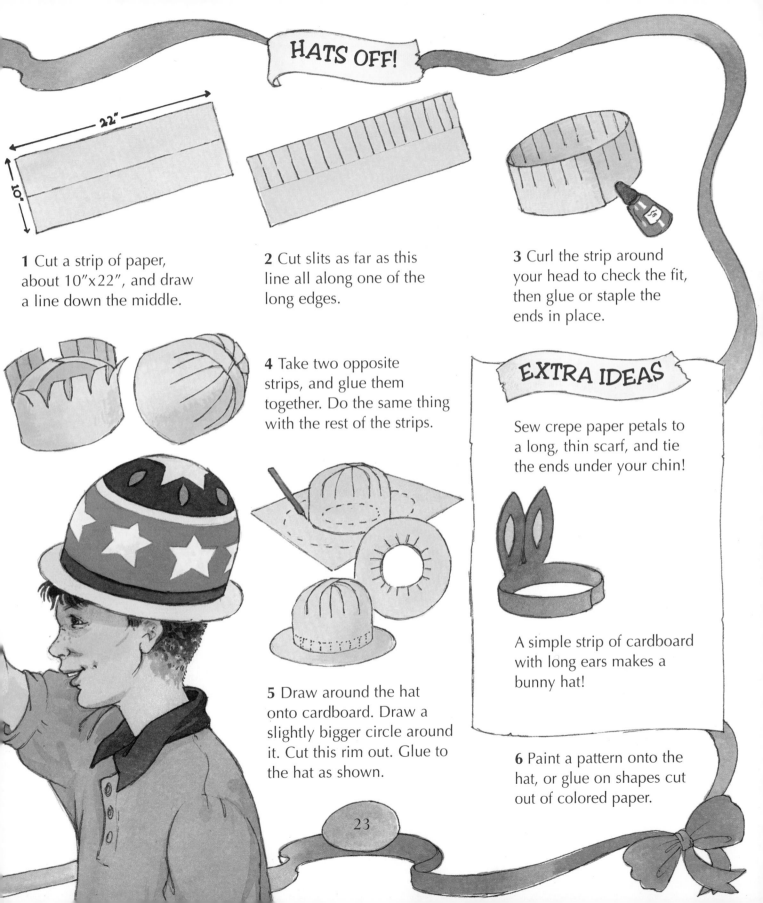

22"

10"

1 Cut a strip of paper, about 10"x22", and draw a line down the middle.

2 Cut slits as far as this line all along one of the long edges.

3 Curl the strip around your head to check the fit, then glue or staple the ends in place.

4 Take two opposite strips, and glue them together. Do the same thing with the rest of the strips.

EXTRA IDEAS

Sew crepe paper petals to a long, thin scarf, and tie the ends under your chin!

A simple strip of cardboard with long ears makes a bunny hat!

5 Draw around the hat onto cardboard. Draw a slightly bigger circle around it. Cut this rim out. Glue to the hat as shown.

6 Paint a pattern onto the hat, or glue on shapes cut out of colored paper.

If there's a light breeze blowing, why not make
and fly this special Easter kite?

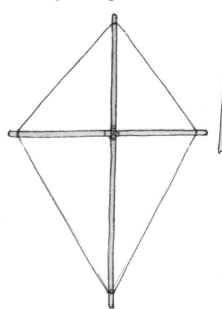

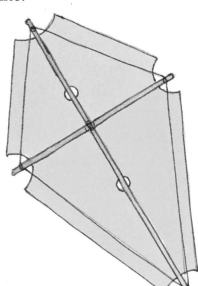

1 Tie the sticks into a
cross with string. Then tie
string from corner to
corner as shown.

2 Put the kite frame onto
the plastic and draw
around it. Draw a border
about 2" wide. Cut two
holes, as shown, and cut
half-circles at each corner.

4 Lay the frame on the
other side and tape the
sides firmly over the string.

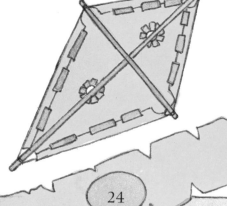

3 Strengthen the holes
and corners with
tape. Then cut your Easter
design out of paper and
glue to one side.

6 Tie the loose end of the spool of string to the middle of the "bridle string."

5 Turn the kite over and tie a piece of string through the two holes to make the "bridle string."

7 Cut a strip of plastic about 40" long. Make cuts along both sides of the strip. Tie one end to the bottom of the kite.

Your kite is now ready to fly! Choose a breezy day and fly it in a wide-open space, far away from trees, buildings, or power lines.

EASTER TRAILS

Here are three different kinds of treasure trails to leave for your family and friends on Easter Sunday—it's up to you what kind of prize they find at the end of it!

TREASURE HUNT

Make a separate trail for each friend, and see who gets to their prize first!

Write out about twelve clues on separate pieces of paper. Each clue will direct your friends to the next one. The final clue tells them where to find their Easter treat!

Don't make it too easy! If the next clue is in an umbrella, you could write "I only go up when something else comes down." Or use a simple code—for example, write all the words and letters backward!

Look inside the bucket

26

PICTURE TRAILS

Divide your friends into teams—each team needs at least two players.

Hide a separate trail for each team. This time the instructions can be quite straightforward. Give one player in each team the first clue, a pad of paper, and a pencil.

The player *draws* the clue on the paper—no words allowed! The rest of the team must look at the drawing to find the next clue. Whoever finds the clue does the next drawing, and so on.

Although each team should be following a separate trail, the final clue should be the same for all teams. The prize goes to the team that was quickest on the draw!

TRACKER TRAIL

Try leaving a secret trail with sticks and stones—work out the signals with a friend so that you both understand it! Here are a few ideas to start you off—try making up some of your own.

straight on

not this way

turn left

turn right

end of the trail

hidden message

27

SPRING CELEBRATIONS

Easter is only one of many springtime festivals that are celebrated around the world. How many others do you know?

Passover is a celebration of freedom. It's the time when Jewish people celebrate the escape of the Israelites from slavery in Egypt, many hundreds of years ago. It is usually celebrated by a special family meal called a Seder.

Purim takes place in February or March. It celebrates the story of Queen Esther, who saved the lives of all the Jews living in Persia (now called Iran). To celebrate this festival, Jewish people in many places have carnivals with big processions—it's a good excuse for both adults and children to put on costumes and dance in the streets!

Mother's Day in the U.S.A. is held on the second Sunday in May. This is the time we thank our mothers for all they do for us during the year, by giving them cards and presents—and maybe some help with the household chores!

April first is a time for tricks and practical jokes. In some parts of the world, you have to play the trick before noon, or the joke's on you!

Holi is an important springtime festival for Hindu people. It's a great time for feasting and merriment—including the custom of throwing colored powder over friends and passersby!

HALLOWEEN FUN

HALLOWEEN HISTORY

The story of Halloween goes all the way back to ancient times. For the Celts who lived in Britain and Ireland at that time, New Year began on November 1. The night before, a festival was held to mark the change from summer to winter.

Because October 31 was the day the sun was at its lowest, it was believed that the sun entered the underworld for a short time, and, while the gates of the underworld were open, evil spirits were released to roam the Earth. To frighten these spirits away, the Celts lit huge bonfires, and dressed up as witches and ghosts.

In time, November 1 became a Christian festival day known as All Saints Day or All Hallows. The night before was called Eve of All Hallows and came to be called Halloween.

Early English settlers brought Halloween customs to the United States, but it was not until the 1800s, when many Irish and Scottish people arrived, that Halloween celebrations became really popular.

Today, most people don't believe in ghosts and witches, but it's fun to dress up as one for a costume party. The most important part of Halloween is to have as good a time as possible!

PARTY PUMPKINS

Without jack-o'-lanterns, Halloween just wouldn't be the same. Jack-o'-lanterns can look spooky or funny, depending on the way you cut your pumpkin. So, ask an adult to help you with the cutting, and follow this easy guide!

Give your pumpkin a smiling or scary face.

1 Get a big pumpkin and cut a circle around the stem. Make the hole big enough to fit your hand in. Scrape out the pumpkin pulp and seeds and save for later.

2 Draw on eyes, nose, and mouth with a pen and cut them out. Keep the face simple to make your lantern more effective.

3 Light a candle and burn a little wax to make a puddle inside the pumpkin. Hold a candle in the puddle until the wax hardens. Ask an adult to help you light it.

CREEPY COSTUMES

A good costume is essential at Halloween, and here are some great ideas for how to make your own. You could be a witch, complete with hat and broom, or maybe you'd like to be a spider — see over the page for the spookiest spider outfit you've ever seen. Also there are ideas on mummy, skeleton, and ghost costumes.

WITCH

You will need

Black fabric, needle and thread, green tinsel, stick-on stars, false nails, cardboard, black paint, a black garbage bag, a wooden pole, twigs, Velcro

2 Decorate the cloak with stick-on stars or glue on cut-out fabric shapes. Sew or glue the tinsel along the front edges of the cloak.

3 Glue on false nails, or paint your own nails a gruesome color.

Make your own magic broom simply by tying a bunch of twigs to a pole with string.

1 Make sure the black fabric is large enough to wrap around you. Sew or glue a 2-inch strip of Velcro tape on both sides of the cloak's neck so you can fasten it.

To make the witch's hat:

1 Cut a brim from the cardboard so the inside circle fits just over your head.

2 Roll another piece of cardboard into a cone shape. The base should fit over the inner circle of the brim.

3 Make small cuts in the brim and stick the tabs to the inside of the cone.

4 Cut a wide strip from a black garbage bag and cut slits along one side.

5 Tape the "hair" into the cone of the hat and trim bangs in front.

SPIDER

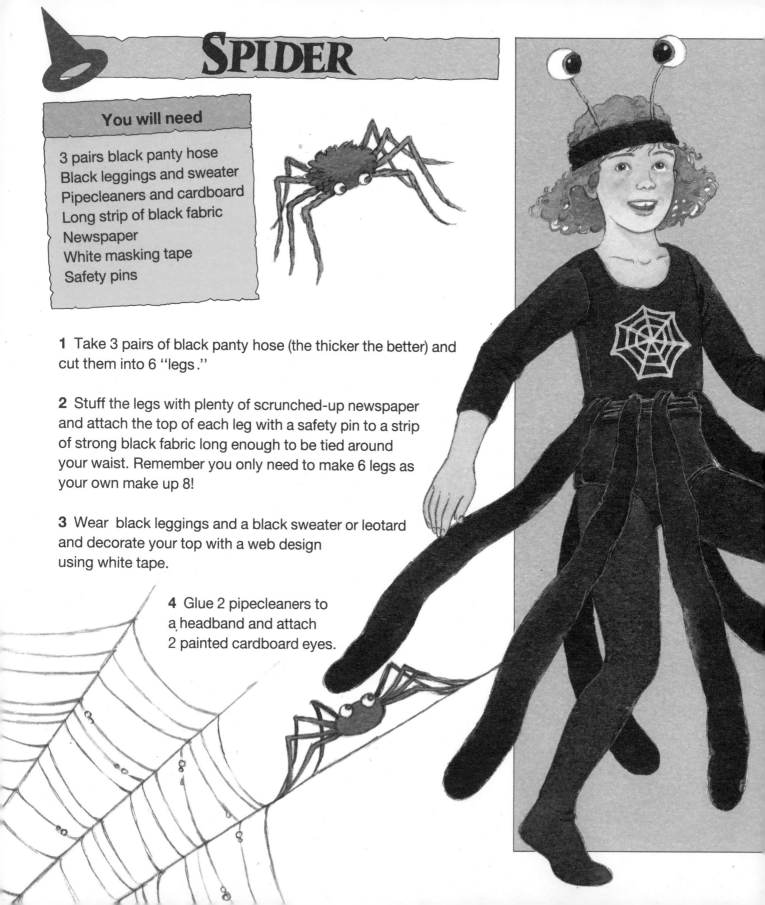

You will need

3 pairs black panty hose
Black leggings and sweater
Pipecleaners and cardboard
Long strip of black fabric
Newspaper
White masking tape
Safety pins

1 Take 3 pairs of black panty hose (the thicker the better) and cut them into 6 "legs."

2 Stuff the legs with plenty of scrunched-up newspaper and attach the top of each leg with a safety pin to a strip of strong black fabric long enough to be tied around your waist. Remember you only need to make 6 legs as your own make up 8!

3 Wear black leggings and a black sweater or leotard and decorate your top with a web design using white tape.

4 Glue 2 pipecleaners to a headband and attach 2 painted cardboard eyes.

◀ To make a slippery bat outfit, cut a black garbage bag along its seams to make it flat; cut along one edge to make bat-shaped wings, and attach to your arms with yarn threaded through the plastic and tied at the elbow.

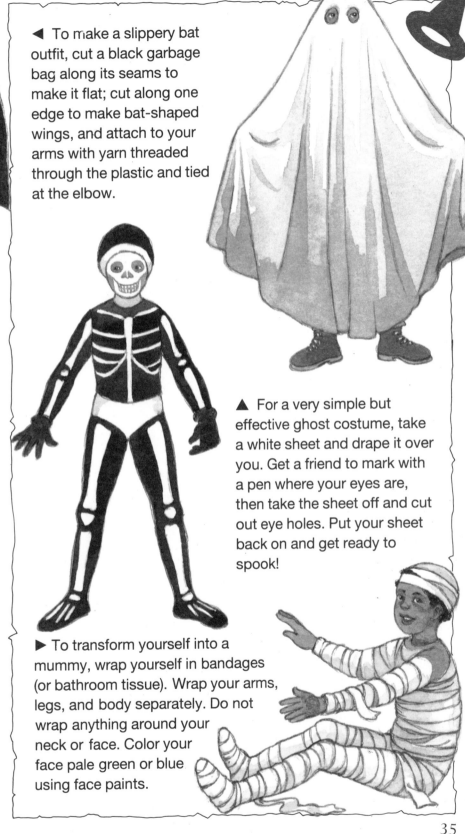

▶ How about being a bony skeleton? You'll need to dress in black and then, using white tape or fabric paint, stick or paint on "bones" — just follow this picture. For a really effective look, paint your face like a skull — see page 37.

▲ For a very simple but effective ghost costume, take a white sheet and drape it over you. Get a friend to mark with a pen where your eyes are, then take the sheet off and cut out eye holes. Put your sheet back on and get ready to spook!

▶ To transform yourself into a mummy, wrap yourself in bandages (or bathroom tissue). Wrap your arms, legs, and body separately. Do not wrap anything around your neck or face. Color your face pale green or blue using face paints.

FEARSOME FACES

To make a good costume look even better, try painting your face to match! Only use face paints — not the ordinary paint that you use for pictures. Use bold strokes, strong colors, and your imagination!

WITCH

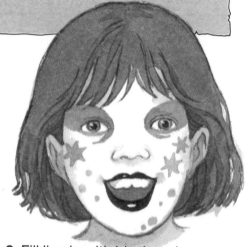

1 Use a white base color all over the face using a damp sponge.

2 Apply purple to the eyes, sweeping the color upward and outward.

3 Fill lips in with black and draw on stars and green warts.

SPIDERWEB

1 Apply white base color with a little pale green color blended around the edges.

2 Draw fine black lines around the eyes and from the nose to the edge of the face.

3 Join the lines with a spiral of black lines. Paint lips black and add a spider.

NIGHT AND DAY

1 Paint one half of your face white and draw a sun and its rays in bright yellow.

2 On the other side, draw a moon above your eye and stars on your cheek in white.

3 Add pale blue clouds to your "daylight" side and color the "night" side dark blue.

For a vampire look, paint the face white with gray shadows around the eyes. Paint eyebrows black and make lips blood red, adding a few red drops on the chin. Finally, paint white fangs.

Frankenstein's monster is recreated using a green base on the face. Draw scars, outline the eyes in black, and paint the mouth blue.

To paint a skeleton face, use black and white face paints and copy the design below.

MONSTROUS MASKS

You need the best possible mask to wear at a Halloween costume party. These pages show you how to make a frighteningly realistic papier-mâché werewolf mask, or if you don't have much time, how to make a simple Dracula cardboard mask. Either way, you'll look sensational!

You will need

A balloon, wallpaper paste, elastic, paints, yarn, newspaper

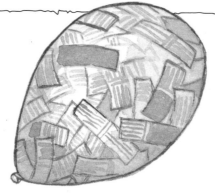

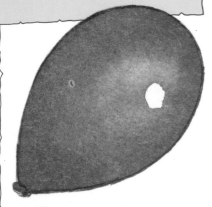

When you have made your basic mask, cut eye and mouth holes and use fresh papier-mâché to build a nose and ears. Then decorate your mask with paints and yarn.

1 Blow up a balloon roughly to your head size.

2 Next, mix wallpaper paste with water.

3 Cut up strips of newspaper and soak in the paste.

4 Cover the balloon evenly with layers of paper strips.

5 When the strips are dry, burst the balloon and cut the paper mold carefully in half with the help of an adult.

6 Make a hole on each side of the mask and thread with elastic.

Trace this mask onto thin cardboard and cut holes for the eyes and mouth. Paint on evil-looking colors and thread elastic through the holes.

39

SCARY SKELETON

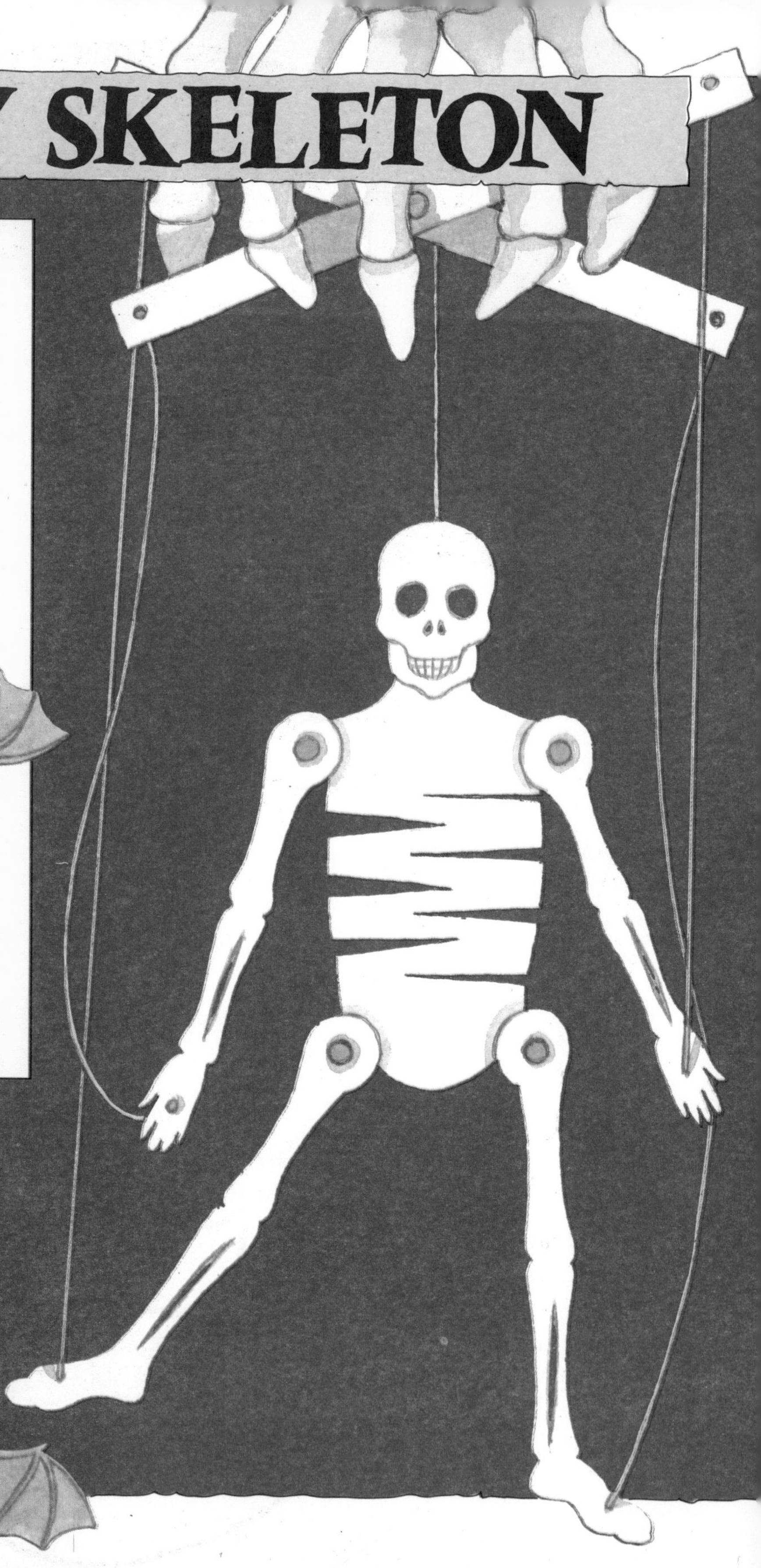

1 First trace all the shapes on the opposite page with a pencil and rub them down onto the cardboard.

You will need

White cardboard
Tracing paper
5 paper fasteners
A needle and thread

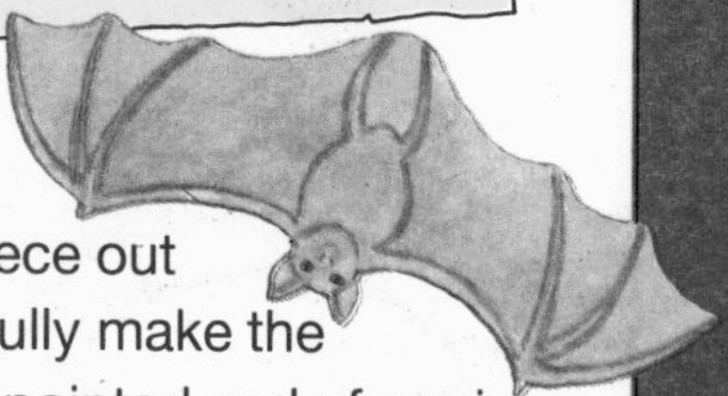

2 Cut each piece out and very carefully make the holes with the pointed end of a pair of scissors.

3 Attach the legs and arms to the body using the fasteners and link the two strips with the fifth fastener. Make sure that each part of the body can move easily.

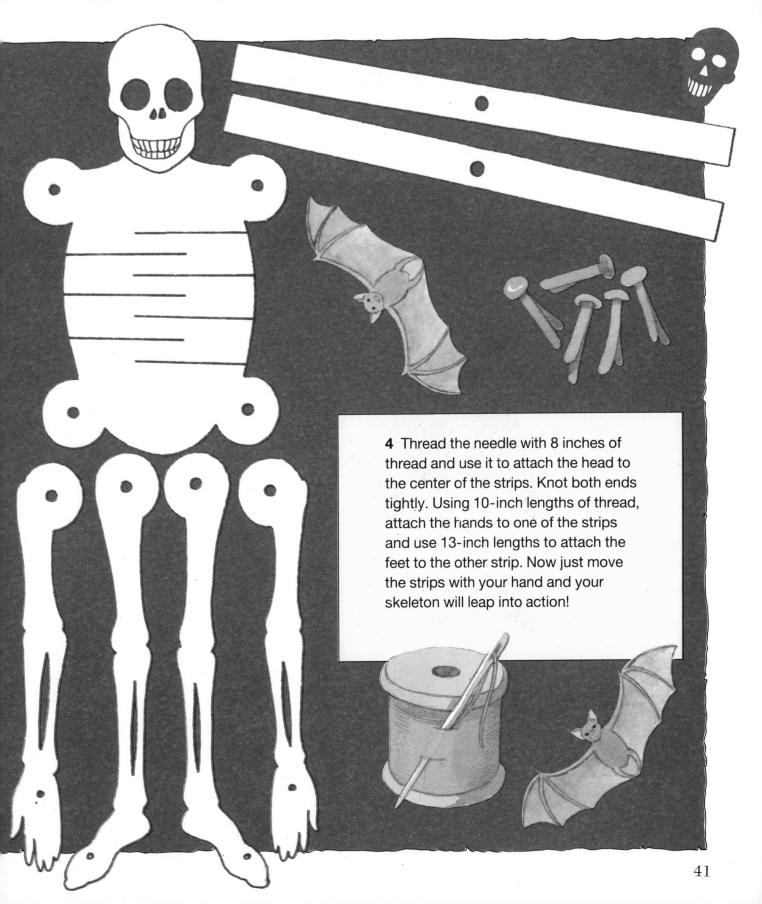

4 Thread the needle with 8 inches of thread and use it to attach the head to the center of the strips. Knot both ends tightly. Using 10-inch lengths of thread, attach the hands to one of the strips and use 13-inch lengths to attach the feet to the other strip. Now just move the strips with your hand and your skeleton will leap into action!

GRUESOME GAMES

Halloween calls for out-of-the-ordinary games to play, so here are some unusual ideas. Invite some friends to join you, and prepare to jump out of your skin!

CRAZY CREATURES

You will need

A spiral-bound notebook
Felt-tip pens
A ruler

1 Draw two lines equally spaced across the first page of your notebook to divide it into three. Do this for at least eight pages, making sure that your lines are in the same place on each page.

2 Draw a different creature on each page, with the head at the top, the body in the middle, and the legs at the bottom.

3 Cut along the lines so you can turn each section on its own. Flip the pages back and forth and make crazy creatures by mixing up heads, bodies, and legs!

VAMPIRE CHASE

This game comes straight from your worst nightmare! You'll need some red stickers, and at least six people. Choose someone to be the vampire (to make them look really convincing, make them the mask on page 39 to wear); everyone else wears three red stickers. The vampire chases its victims around and, if someone is caught, the vampire takes a drop of blood (a red sticker). When someone loses all three stickers, they become the vampire—and so the game continues . . .

GHOSTLY GROANS

You'll need a large space for this ghoulish game and again, six people or more. Pick a "ghost hunter" and blindfold him or her. The other players or "ghosts" circle around the ghost hunter who must try to catch one of them. When someone is caught they must wail and moan in as ghostly a way as possible and the ghost hunter must guess who it is. If the ghost hunter guesses correctly he or she can change places with the ghost they caught. If not, the ghost goes free and the ghost hunter must try again.

DEVILICIOUS CAKES

A witch's kitchen is never busier than at Halloween, and a really special party cake is fun to make and even better to eat! Ask an adult to help, and follow the recipe below for a delicious chocolate Witch's Cat Cake, or try making a cake in the shape of a bat or spiderweb...

You will need

A rectangular cake pan
13 × 9 × 2 inches
1 cup butter or margarine
1 cup superfine sugar
3 eggs
2 cups self-rising flour
2 tablespoons cocoa
4 mini jelly rolls
Licorice and green candy

For the Icing:
$1\frac{1}{2}$ cups confectioners' sugar
2 tablespoons cocoa
2 tablespoons hot water
$\frac{1}{4}$ cup butter or margarine
1 teaspoon vanilla extract
Chocolate sprinkles

1 Preheat oven to 350°F. Beat butter and sugar together in a mixing bowl until creamy. Add beaten egg gradually and then the cocoa (mixed with hot water). Sift the flour into the mixture until it is soft and light.

2 Line the pan with waxed paper and pour mixture evenly into it. Bake for about 30 minutes.

3 Allow your cake to cool on a wire rack. Then cut out a basic cat shape as shown. Use the spare cake to make wedge-shaped ears.

4 To make the icing, simply sift the confectioners' sugar and cocoa into a bowl, and gradually mix in the soft butter, water, and vanilla extract, until the icing is creamy. Spread thickly onto the cat shape. Position the ears firmly and cover with icing. Shake a layer of chocolate sprinkles over as a finishing touch.

44

5 To make the cat's tail, stick the jelly rolls together and to the "body" with a little icing and cut the end of the "tail" at an angle to form a point. Cover the tail with icing.

6 Use licorice candy for whiskers and finally, green candy to make a pair of glowing eyes!

For the bat and spiderweb cakes use the same recipe. Make 2 round cakes, sandwich them together with chocolate icing, and cover with the same icing.

To make a bat, cut the round cake into a bat shape and decorate with licorice candy.

Create a spiderweb design, by making some white icing from confectioners' sugar and a little water. Dribble the white icing in a spiral shape then draw lines from the center outward using a toothpick. Add a toy spider!

SPOOKY SOUNDS

Scary movies without spooky sounds wouldn't be scary at all — that's how important it is to create the right noises if you want to have a really eerie Halloween evening. If you have a tape recorder, try recording your own scary sound effects using the tricks shown here. Watch your friends' faces when you secretly play the tape back to them . . .

Rumbling Thunder

Take a large sheet of stiff cardboard. Holding it by the edges, shake it back and forth so that the middle part wobbles. This makes a rumbling thunder noise.

Hooting Owl

For a haunting owl hoot blow gently across the top of an empty bottle.
To make higher or lower hoots, you can blow across bottles containing different levels of water.

Creaks and Squeaks

Try opening a stiff door as slowly as you can for a haunted house sound effect. Or run your finger around the rim of a half-filled glass of water to make a strange, wailing noise. Shake a bag of dead leaves for a rustling effect. Often the best sounds are made with your own voice — try a cackling giggle or a deep-voiced laugh . . .

Horses' Hooves

For the chilling sound of a phantom horse use 2 empty yogurt containers or plastic flowerpots. Tap them on a table to make a hollow clopping sound.

SPOOKY SHADOWS

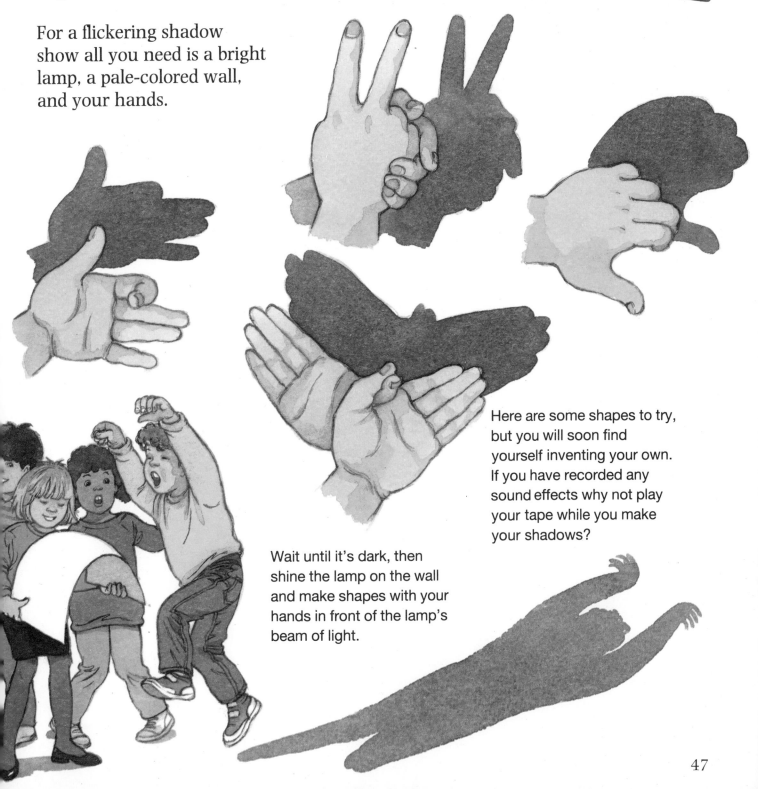

For a flickering shadow show all you need is a bright lamp, a pale-colored wall, and your hands.

Here are some shapes to try, but you will soon find yourself inventing your own. If you have recorded any sound effects why not play your tape while you make your shadows?

Wait until it's dark, then shine the lamp on the wall and make shapes with your hands in front of the lamp's beam of light.

POEMS FOR HALLOWEEN

Nothing is scarier than a spooky tale read aloud on Halloween night. Here are some poems that will send shivers down your spine. Or, why not write some yourself with mysterious invisible ink. Just dip a pen with a nib into the cut half of a lemon and write your poem. To make the writing visible, hold the paper up against a warm radiator.

The Moon

The moon has a face like the clock in the hall;
She shines on thieves on the garden wall,
On streets and fields and harbor quays,
And birdies asleep in the forks of the trees.

The squalling cat and the squeaking mouse,
The howling dog by the door of the house,
The bat that lies in bed at noon,
All love to be out by the light of the moon.

ROBERT LOUIS STEVENSON

In the dark, dark wood, there was
a dark, dark house,
And in that dark, dark house, there was
a dark, dark room,
And in that dark, dark room, there was
a dark, dark cupboard,
And in that dark, dark cupboard, there was
a dark, dark shelf,
And on that dark, dark shelf, there was
a dark, dark, box,
And in that dark, dark box, there was
a GHOST!

ANON.

A skeleton once in Khartoum
Invited a ghost to his room.
They spent the whole night
In the eeriest fight
As to which should be frightened of whom.

Song of the Witches

Double, double toil and trouble;
Fire burn and caldron bubble.
Fillet of a fenny snake,
In the caldron boil and bake;
Eye of newt and toe of frog,
Wool of bat and tongue of dog,
Adder's fork and blindworm's sting,
Lizard's leg and howlet's wing,
For a charm of powerful trouble,
Like a hell-broth boil and bubble.

Double, double toil and trouble;
Fire burn and caldron bubble.
Cool it with a baboon's blood,
Then the charm is firm and good.

WILLIAM SHAKESPEARE

Witches fly skyward
Into the blackness,
Their passengers always
Cats of the darkest.
Halloween is with us,
Eve of All Saints, and
Spirits are stirring.

JOHN PATON

Queen Nefertiti

Spin a coin, spin a coin,
        All fall down;
Queen Nefertiti
        Stalks through the town.

Over the sidewalks
        Her feet go clack
Her legs are as tall
        As a chimney stack

Her fingers flicker
        Like snakes in the air,
The walls split open
        At her green-eyed stare;

Her voice is thin
        As the ghosts of bees;
She will crumble your bones,
        She will make your blood freeze.

Spin a coin, spin a coin,
        All fall down;
Queen Nefertiti
        Stalks through the town.

ANON.

GHOULISH GREETINGS

Whoever gets this card is in for a shocking surprise! The card fits flat into an envelope and pops up to frighten the wits out of the (un)lucky person who opens it.

You will need

Thin cardboard, felt-tip pens, medium-sized rubber band

1 Copy the design on the right onto the cardboard at the measurements given.

2 Color the witch's head and cut the card out. Cut the oblong hole in the middle of the card, making sure that it is slightly wider than the witch's head.

3 Fold the card along the dotted lines, folding away from you. Push the head through the hole as you fold.

4 Loop one end of the rubber band over the notches at the back, and the other end over the notches at the bottom. This is the tricky part — ask an adult to help if you find it difficult.

5 To put the card into the envelope, squeeze it lightly together so that the rubber band stretches and the card becomes flat. It will spring back into terrifying shape the moment the envelope is opened!

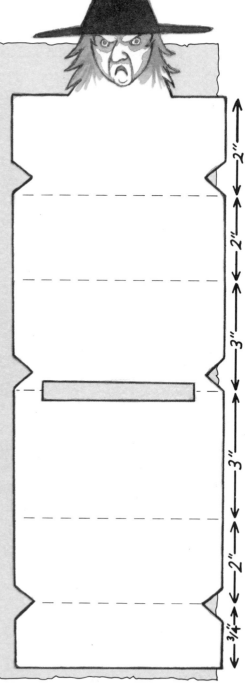

THANKSGIVING FUN

The Story of Thanksgiving

In December, 1620, a ship called the *Mayflower* landed in Plymouth Harbor, Massachusetts. On board were 102 Puritans. Calling themselves Pilgrims, they had come from England to seek religious freedom in the New World.

The Pilgrims faced great hardships in their first year. Food was scarce, and many died of hunger and disease. But the Native Americans helped them hunt and fish, and taught them to plant corn, pumpkins, and squash.

After their first harvest was gathered, the Pilgrims held a festival of Thanksgiving, with prayers, games, and a huge feast. They invited the Native Americans, who brought deer and turkeys.

In 1863, President Lincoln declared the last Thursday in November an official Thanksgiving holiday. Now, like the Pilgrims, we celebrate Thanksgiving with fun and feasting.

The First Thanksgiving

When the Pilgrims
first gathered together to share
with their Indian friends
in the mild autumn air,
they lifted their voices
in jubilant praise
for the bread on the table,
the berries and maize,
for field and for forest
for turkey and deer,
for the bountiful crops
they were blessed with that year.
They were thankful for these
as they feasted away,
and as they were thankful,
we're thankful today.

JACK PRELUTSKY

Thanksgiving Greetings

It's fun to send greeting cards, especially when you've made them yourself. Your friends will love this card, with its pop-up surprise!

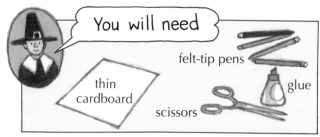

You will need

felt-tip pens

thin cardboard

scissors

glue

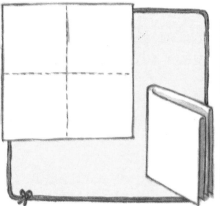

1. Cut out a large square from a sheet of thin cardboard. Fold in half, then in half again.

2. Use a ruler to draw a line across the folded corner to make a triangle. Fold toward the opposite corner.

3. Open out and color the diamond shape red. Fold in half and cut along the center fold to the triangle tip.

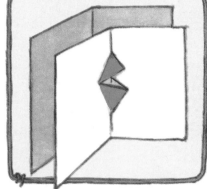

4. Fold the red part to make a beak, and tuck inside. Fold another cardboard square in half, and decorate.

5. Glue both pieces together. *Don't* glue the back of the beak! Finish the inside design and sign!

You're Invited!

Make your Thanksgiving Day guests feel really special by sending them these custom-made, stand-up invitations.

1. Fold a piece of cardboard in half, open out, and draw a Thanksgiving picture that extends over the top half.

2. Carefully cut around the outside of the picture on the top half only. (You may want to ask an adult to help.)

3. Write your invitation on the inside. When the card is folded, the picture will stand up!

A Harvest Collage

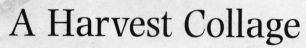

There are lots of ways you can help make your home look bright and festive for the Thanksgiving holiday. This fall collage, made from dried grass, leaves, cranberries, seeds, and beans, will look beautiful anywhere in the house!

You will need

cardboard
cranberries
dried beans
seeds (such as pumpkin and sunflower)
bark
leaves
glue
dried grass

1. If you like, give your collage a background color by painting the cardboard—but make sure the paint is dry before the next step!

2. Lightly sketch in your picture in pencil, and begin gluing your materials in place. Work in small areas, filling them in closely.

3. To make the apple tree shown here, you can use bark for the tree trunk, real leaves, and cranberries.

Try thinking up your own ideas for designs and materials to use. Look for interesting colors and textures—let your imagination take over!

Super Streamers

These streamers are fun to make and look great in a window, above your bed, or even strung across the Thanksgiving table. To make the streamers really eye-catching, use bright fall colors. Take care when cutting around your turkey or leaf shape.

1. Fold a strip of crepe paper accordion-style. Make sure the sections are equal, and big enough for you to draw on.

2. On the top sheet, draw a simple turkey or leaf shape like the ones shown here. It must go all the way out to the edges.

3. Keeping the paper folded, cut around the shape. Be sure to leave some of each folded side uncut, or your streamer will fall apart.

Frame Your Family!

Thanksgiving has always been a holiday to share with those we love. We celebrate the joy of being together, and give thanks for our families and friends.

Here's a wonderful gift you can make for your family, so that everyone remembers this Thanksgiving as an extra-special one. First, go out and gather some colorful autumn leaves. If they're not completely flat, you can put them between sheets of tissue or newspaper and press them between the pages of a heavy book. Next, find some family photos to copy, and draw or paint a family portrait. Don't forget to include yourself! Now, here's how to make a beautiful autumn-leaf frame for your portrait.

You will need

4 strips of heavy cardboard, about 2 inches wide
ruler
tape
scissors
glue
craft knife (an adult should help)
varnish

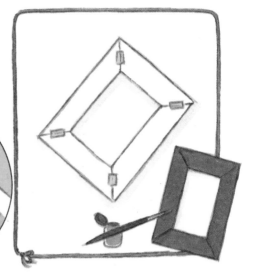

1. Cut two long and two short cardboard strips, to measure 2 inches longer than your picture. Tape them together at the corners.

2. Neaten the corners by cutting diagonally and fitting them together. Secure with tape. Paint the frame a dark color.

MAPLE

OAK

HORSE CHESTNUT

SUMAC

3. Glue the leaves to the cardboard and then varnish the frame. Tape your picture securely to the back of the frame.

4. To make a stand for the picture, cut out a cardboard wedge and tape it to the back of the frame.

Decorate the Table!

Here are some ideas to help give your Thanksgiving table a really festive look. Use brightly colored autumn leaves to make these lovely place mats and napkin rings. The cheerful turkey place cards will add a special finishing touch!

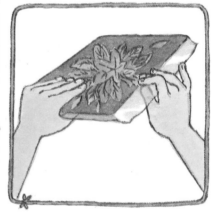

You will need

- leaves
- cardboard
- glue
- clear contact paper
- aluminum foil
- cardboard tube
- paint
- scissors
- felt-tip pens and crayons
- thin paper

Place Mats

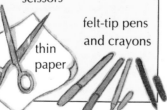

1. Use one sheet of heavy cardboard for each mat. Glue on leaves in interesting patterns and different color combinations.

2. Using a sheet of contact paper 1½ inches larger overall than your mat, carefully cover the mat. Trim any excess paper.

Napkin Rings

For each napkin ring, you'll need a strip of foil 7 inches long by 3 inches wide.

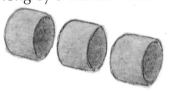

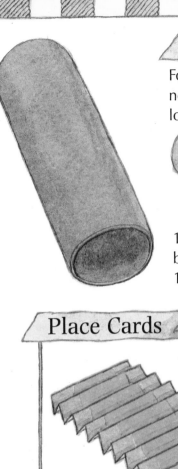

1. Cut the cardboard tube into 1-inch sections.

2. Wrap the foil around the ring and press firmly.

3. Where the foil ends overlap, glue on a small leaf.

Place Cards

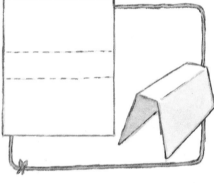

1. Use a sheet of thin paper about 5 x 11 inches. Paint as shown, then make narrow accordion folds.

2. Holding the folded strips flat, fold in half and glue together in the middle. Fan out the "tail feathers."

3. To make the card, fold a piece of thin cardboard (5 x 7 inches) in two places as shown.

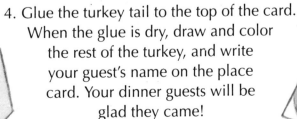

4. Glue the turkey tail to the top of the card. When the glue is dry, draw and color the rest of the turkey, and write your guest's name on the place card. Your dinner guests will be glad they came!

Gorgeous Gifts

If you've been invited to Thanksgiving dinner, you might want to take a gift for your host or hostess. This Indian- corn wreath, with its warm fall colors, is a perfect Thanksgiving Day present to hang on the front door!

You will need

- paint
- knitting needle
- brush
- picture wire
- elastic thread
- Indian corn
- needle
- clear nail polish
- cranberries
- pumpkin seeds

Corn Wreath

1. Ask an adult to cut the corn into 2-inch sections. With the knitting needle, poke a hole through them.

2. Thread the corn onto the picture wire. Form a circle and fasten the ends. Decorate with dried flowers.

This bracelet and necklace set, made from pumpkin seeds and cranberries, is great for Thanksgiving giving!

Joyful Jewelry

1. Carefully paint the seeds in bright colors. When the paint is dry, seal it with a coat of clear nail polish.

2. Thread the seeds and cranberries alternately on lengths of elastic thread, then tie the ends securely.

Wrap It Up!

If you're giving gifts at Thanksgiving, you'll want to wrap them as attractively as possible. It's easy and fun to design and print your own wrapping paper—and it will make your gifts even more special! Here are some autumnal ideas for you to try, but you'll soon find yourself thinking up new Thanksgiving shapes and colors.

You will need

plain brown wrapping paper
poster paints
apples or potatoes
leaves
paintbrush
knife (see safety note)

Decide what colors you want to use for your prints, and pour some of each color into a separate saucer. The paint shouldn't be too thick—dilute with water if necessary.

To make turkey designs, dip your hand in paint and make hand prints all over the paper. Using your thumbprint as the turkey's neck and head, paint in eyes, beaks, and legs.

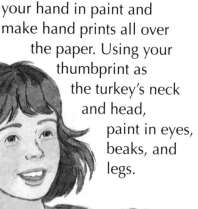

Never use knives without the help of an adult.

Safety Note

1. Cut an apple or potato in half. Lightly draw a simple shape onto the flat part of the fruit or vegetable.

2. Cut around the shape so it forms a raised surface. Dip it into paint and press firmly onto a large sheet of paper.

Leaf printing

Leaf prints in bright fall colors make especially pretty wrapping paper designs.

1. Collect leaves in as many different shapes, colors, and sizes as you can find.

2. Gently dip each leaf into the paint, making sure the paint is not mixed too thinly.

3. Press the leaf down firmly and lift up carefully.

Wrap your presents with ribbons to match your printed designs, and the packages will be as beautiful as the presents themselves!

Thanksgiving Treats

One of the best things about Thanksgiving, of course, is eating! Here are some easy-to-fix, tempting treats you can make for the Thanksgiving dinner table, or for enjoying anytime over the Thanksgiving holiday.

Cranberry Punch

cranberry juice
ginger ale

apple juice
lemon slices

1. Make flavored ice cubes: dilute fruit juice or ginger ale with water.

2. Fill an ice cube tray and freeze. Put cubes into a large pitcher.

3. Pour equal amounts of juice and ginger ale into the pitcher.

4. Carefully cut some lemon slices to add to your punch.

Quick Cranberry Relish

2 cups of fresh cranberries
¼ cup orange juice
¼ cup water 1 cup sugar

1. Heat in a saucepan over a medium flame, stirring gently, for about 7–10 minutes until the cranberries pop open. Make sure an adult helps you use the stove.

2. Cool and serve with your Thanksgiving turkey. Yum!

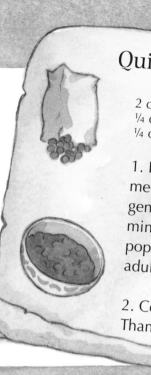

Corny Cupcakes

1 cup flour   ½ cup sugar
¼ cup soft butter   1 egg
¼ cup milk   1 tsp. salt
1 tsp. baking powder
Ready-made frosting
Candy corn to decorate

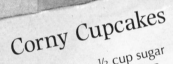

1. Ask an adult to preheat the oven to 375° F.

2. Sift the flour and sugar together into a mixing bowl.

3. Add the butter, milk, egg, sugar, salt, and baking powder. Beat until the mixture is smooth.

4. Pour into a muffin tin lined with cupcake liners. Put the tin into the oven for about 20 minutes.

5. When cool, spread frosting on top of the cupcakes and decorate with candy corn.

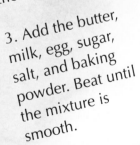

Thanksgiving Journey

Thanksgiving is a day for sharing, and many people travel thousands of miles just to be with their families at this special time. This poem, written more than a hundred years ago, is about one family's journey.

Thanksgiving Day

Over the river and through the wood,
    To Grandfather's house we go;
        The horse knows the way
        To carry the sleigh
    Through the white and drifted snow.

Over the river and through the wood—
    Oh, how the wind does blow!
        It stings the toes
        And bites the nose
    As over the ground we go.

Over the river and through the wood,
    To have a first-rate play.
        Hear the bells ring,
        "Ting-a-ling-ding!"
    Hurrah for Thanksgiving Day!

Over the river and through the wood,
Trot fast, my dapple-gray!
Spring over the ground
Like a hunting hound,
For this is Thanksgiving Day!

Over the river and through the wood,
And straight through the barnyard gate.
We seem to go
Extremely slow—
It is so hard to wait!

Over the river and through the wood—
Now Grandmother's cap I spy!
Hurrah for the fun!
Is the pudding done?
Hurrah for the pumpkin pie!

LYDIA MARIA CHILD

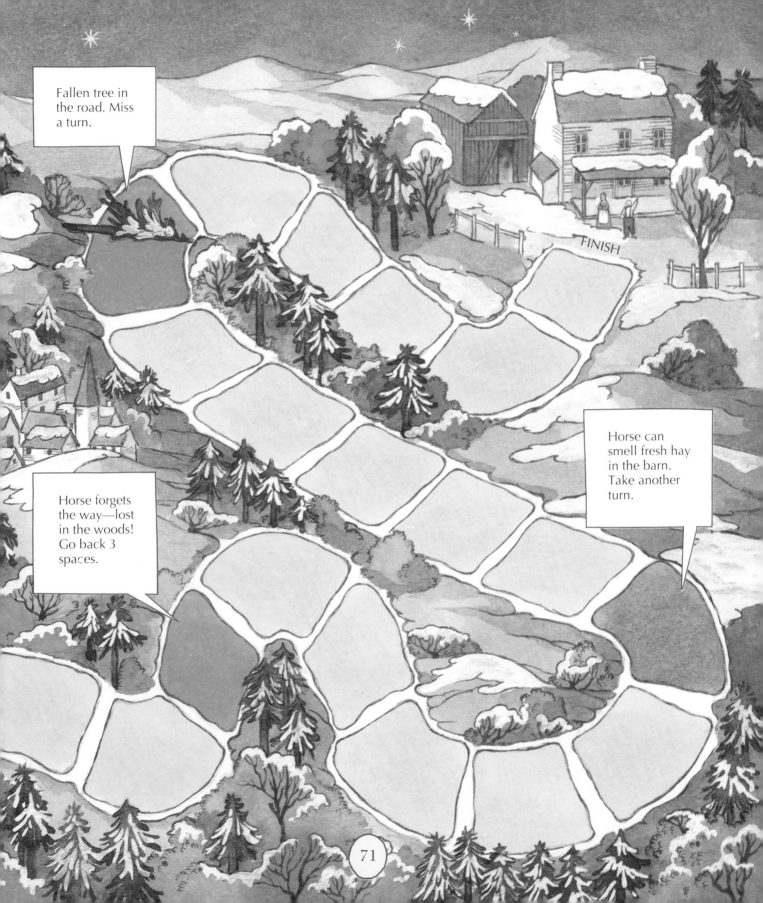

All Around the World

In Canada, Thanksgiving is celebrated just as it is in the United States, but on a different day—the second Monday in October. There are thanksgiving festivals in other parts of the world, too. Throughout history, people of every culture and religion have come together to give thanks at harvest time.

GREAT BRITAIN
Harvest festival takes place in late September or October. Churches are decorated with autumn flowers, and with fruits, vegetables, and other food. A special service of thanksgiving is held in the church on a Sunday.

CHINA
Zhong Qui, or the Festival of the Autumn Moon, is held in the 8th month of the Chinese calendar. Mooncakes are offered to the Moon Goddess, and in the evening children parade with colored lanterns.

JUDAISM WORLD-WIDE

The festival of *Sukkot* lasts for nine days. Jewish families build a temporary booth called a *sukka*, which is decorated with leaves, branches, and newly harvested fruits and vegetables. Prayers are said and meals are eaten in the *sukka*.

INDIA

The harvest festival of *Onam* is celebrated in the state of Kerala, in southern India. Homes are decorated with flowers, and food is distributed to the poor and needy. There are more festivities in the evening, including fireworks.

LITHUANIA

During harvest celebrations in this part of eastern Europe, the last sheaf of grain is dressed up with ribbons and flowers to make a doll called a *boba*, or "old woman." The *boba* is kept until spring, so that the spirit of the crop stays alive until replanting.

Turkey Tomfoolery

When is a Turkey scary?

When it's a-goblin'!

What language do turkeys speak?

Gobble-de-gook!

Why did the turkey cross the road?

To visit the chicken on the other side.

THANKSGIVING WORD CHALLENGE

How many words of 4 letters or more (not counting plurals) can you make from the letters in THANKSGIVING? There are at least 40—answers below. (No peeking!)

asking	king	shin	tank	visit
gain	knight	sigh	task	vista
gait	knit	sight	than	
gang	night	sing	thank	
gnat	saint	sink	thin	
hang	sang	skin	thing	
hank	sank	snag	think	
having	satin	stain	vain	
hint	saving	stink	vanish	
insight	shaving	tang	vast	

HANUKKAH FUN

ABOUT HANUKKAH

Hanukkah is a festival of light and giving. It is celebrated by Jewish people all over the world. For eight days and nights candles are lit, and gifts are exchanged to celebrate a miracle that happened a long time ago in Judea—the land we now call Israel.

THE STORY OF HANUKKAH

More than 2,000 years ago the land of Judea was ruled by the Syrian king, Antiochus. He commanded that all the Jews in his kingdom were no longer to worship just one god but instead must convert to the Greek religion and worship many gods. Antiochus filled the holy temple in Jerusalem (the capital city of Judea) with idols and statues, and ordered the Jewish people to worship them.

If anyone disobeyed, Antiochus commanded his troops to set fire to their towns and villages and even to kill them! In the town of Modi'in lived Mattathias, a priest who led the Jewish resistance against Antiochus.

Mattathias fled with his family to live in the hills. Other Jewish families followed and a community was settled. Mattathias chose his son Judah Maccabee to lead this community. Judah formed a small army known as the Maccabees who were trained to surprise the Syrian army at night. After three long years, they won their battle and set about restoring the holy temple in Jerusalem. A special menorah was made for the temple, and enough oil was found to light the menorah for one day. But to everyone's amazement, the oil kept on burning—for eight days and nights! The miracle of Hanukkah was born . . . .

YOUR HANUKKIAH

A hanukkiah is a menorah used especially at Hanukkah. It holds nine candles and is the center of all the celebrations during this time. Each night, for eight nights, another candle is lit from one special candle—the Shamash, which means "helper." By the eighth day, all the candles have been lit. Try making your own hanukkiah, using clay, paint, and glue. Remember to make sure that the paint and glue you buy is safe to burn, and ask an adult to help with gluing and varnishing.

You will need

small pack (1lb) of DAS clay, gold acrylic paint, blunt knife, 9 candles, clear varnish, rolling pin and board, paint brushes, old newspaper or sheets of plastic

SIMPLE HANUKKIAH

1 Organize your work surface by covering a table with sheets of old newspaper or plastic.

2 Divide the clay into four equal lumps.

3 Roll out each lump into a long tube shape.

4 Twist two clay tubes to make a loose chain. Add a candle to each twist until you have put in nine candles. Twist the other two clay tubes over the first two for the second layer.

5 Gently press the two layers together and trim off the extra clay.

6 Roll your trimmings into another, shorter, tube and wind this gently around the first candle only. This makes a third layer for the Shamash—the candle you use to light all the other candles.

7 Place your hanukkiah in a warm place to dry out for a couple of days. Now you're ready to take out the candles and paint the hanukkiah gold. When the paint is dry, ask an adult to help you put a coat of varnish on it. Leave it to dry completely before you light the first candle for Hanukkah.

A HANUKKIAH TREE

This hanukkiah is made in the more traditional menorah shape.

You will need

large pack (2 lb) DAS clay, blunt knife, strong glue (Elmer's), blue and gold acrylic paints (or any other colors you like), clear varnish, old newspaper or plastic sheets, rolling pin and board

1 As before, prepare your work surface. Lay sheets of old newspaper or plastic over a table top.

2 ▶ Roll out the clay into a round, flat disk. Roll it until it is about one inch thick and twelve inches across.

3 ▼ Cut the shapes, below, out of the clay with the tip of your blunt knife, making sure that all the pieces are flat. Put the leftover clay aside.

4 ▼ Push the handle of your knife into the tops of the branches and the stem to make holes for the candles.

5 ▶ Leave the pieces of your tree to dry in a warm place for at least two days. Keep turning them over—gently—until they are completely dry. Then glue all the connecting pieces together— very carefully—until you have a complete "tree."

7 ▶ Now lay your hanukkiah down on old newspaper and leave it so that the glue can dry. Once the glue has set firm, you can start painting—how about deep blue, or bright pink?

8 ▼ Make small decorative shapes with leftover clay. When they are dry, paint them, let the paint dry, and glue them onto your hanukkiah. Finally, ask an adult to cover your hanukkiah with a coat of varnish. . .magnificent!

CRAZY CANDLES

It's simple and fun decorating candles for a hanukkiah, or for around your home. Make sure you *always* ask an adult to light the candles, and check carefully that your paints and glue are safe to burn. Crayons, acrylic paint, and glitter are usually safe.

CRAYON CANDLES

An easy way to decorate your candles is to use melted crayons.

1 Put a plain candle in the candle holder and ask an adult to light it.

2 Keeping your fingers out of reach of the flame, hold a crayon over the candle, and let it drip onto the candle below.

You will need

colored crayons
plain white candles
a candle holder

You can make patterns using different colored crayons—dots, stripes, and so on. See how many different patterns you can make!

PAINTED CANDLES

It's hard finding things that will stick to the slippery surface of the candles, but acrylic paint does and is very easy to use. Here are some ideas for decorating your candles using acrylic paints.

You will need

acrylic paints
paint brushes
an old plate
a candle holder
glitter, sequins

1 Stand the candles in a hanukkiah, or candle holder, so you don't get messy hands!

2 Using your paints, paint whatever design you like on your candle.

SPARKLING CANDLES

1 ▼ Pour some glitter onto a plate. Paint a candle, and roll it in the glitter.

2 ▼ Add sequins to your glitter for extra sparkle!

3 For textured candles, make a mix of paint and glitter. Roll your candle in the mixture!

BAKE A DREIDEL

This salt-dough dreidel looks stunning as a table or mantel decoration . . . .

You will need

1 cup of flour, half cup of salt, tablespoon of cooking oil, half cup of water, plastic bag, baking sheet, white glue, clear acrylic varnish, glitter glue in bright colors, felt-tip pen

SALT DOUGH

Mix the flour, salt, oil, and water together in a bowl until a dough is formed. Knead the dough on a work surface for a few minutes until it is smooth. Place the salt dough in a plastic bag to keep it from drying out until you're ready to use it.

MAKING THE DREIDEL

1 ▸ Ask an adult to preheat the oven to 200°F. Roll the salt dough into a tube shape, about two inches across.

2 ▸ Form into a cube by pressing each side onto the work surface. Then pull the dough out at one end to make a handle.

3 ▸ Form the other end of the cube into a point. Place on a baking sheet, and ask an adult to put it in the oven for two hours.

2 in.

4 ▾ When it is baked dry and has completely cooled, ask an adult to help paint it with a coat of varnish. Leave it to dry, resting it over an old mug or glass.

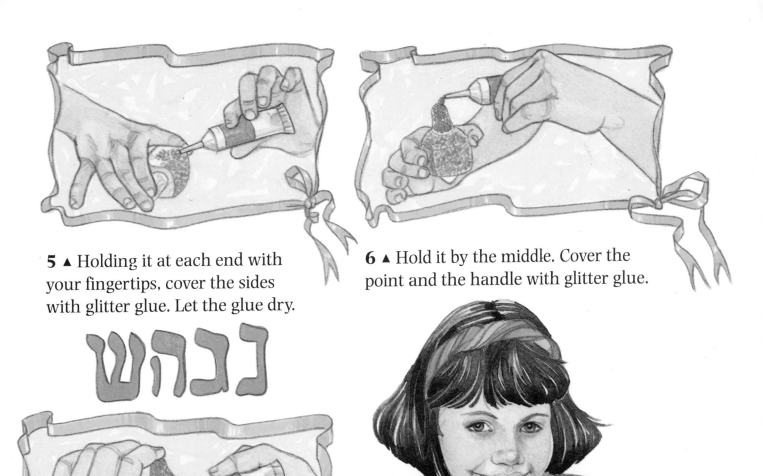

5 ▲ Holding it at each end with your fingertips, cover the sides with glitter glue. Let the glue dry.

6 ▲ Hold it by the middle. Cover the point and the handle with glitter glue.

שהגנ

7 ▲ When the dreidel is dry, write Hebrew letters with a felt-tip pen on the sides, in the order shown above. (To find out what these letters mean, turn to page 96). Go over them with colored glitter glue. Wait for each letter to dry before going on to the next one.

8 Finally, ask an adult to cover the dreidel with a coat of varnish. Leave it to dry.

RINGING DREIDEL

This felt dreidel makes a great toy for a brother or sister—or you can use it to play the dreidel game on the next page.

You will need

a sheet of medium thick cardboard, paper, felt-tip pens, blunt scissors, ruler, toy bell, wooden chopstick (painted gold), fabric glue, different colored felt, craft paper

1 ▼ Using the measurements shown, copy this shape onto cardboard and cut it out. Fold along the dotted lines, and glue down all the flaps except the top one.

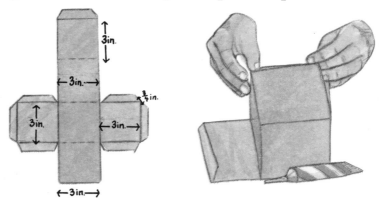

3in.

3in.

3in.

3in.

3/4 in.

3in.

2 ▼ Put your bell inside, through the top of the cube, and glue down the top flap.

3 Cut out six three-inch felt squares in different colors. Glue a square onto each side of the cube. Make a hole at each end and push the chopstick through. Seal in place with a dab of glue.

4 Trace onto paper and cut out the four Hebrew letters on page 96. These will be your patterns. Tape them to felt, and cut out the felt letters. Glue the felt letters onto the sides of your cube.

Now you're ready to play Spin the Dreidel. You need between two and eight friends, sitting in a circle. Give each player an equal number of candies, fruit, nuts, or coins. Place a plate in the middle. Use your felt dreidel to play. Here is what the Hebrew letters mean in this game:

Nun means take nothing from the plate.
Gimel means take all.
Heh means take half.
Shin means put something on the plate.

SPIN THE DREIDEL

Each player puts the same amount of candies, nuts, etc., onto the plate, and spins the dreidel once. When it stops, the letter on top tells the player what to do.

The winner is the one who has the biggest pile when the plate is empty!

EXCELLENT OILS

Turn olive oil into tasty flavored herbal oil that the whole family will enjoy. . . .

You will need

olive oil, peppercorns, garlic, herbs (bay leaves, basil, sage, tarragon, rosemary, or oregano), old salad dressing bottles or jars with lids or corks, rubber gloves, sticky labels, felt-tip pens

HERBAL OIL

1 Thoroughly wash and dry the old bottles or jars.

2 Choose which herb you want to use—try individual herbs, or combine them with garlic and peppercorns.

3 Wearing rubber gloves, push the flavorings into the bottle and fill it up with olive oil. Replace the lid or cork tightly.

4 Wipe any spilled oil off the bottle and dry it. Label the oil with the ingredients you've used.

SWEET SCENTED OIL

These scented herbal oils are *not* for cooking or swallowing—you put them in the bathtub! Different oils are good for different reasons—rosemary can help wake you up if you're feeling tired, while geranium and lavender are cooling and calming.

You will need

almond oil, a selection of oils such as rosemary, lavender, or geranium (ask an adult to buy these), small plastic or glass bottles with lids or corks, labels, a small funnel, felt-tip pens, rubber gloves

1 ▼ Fill the bottles almost to the top with almond oil. Add drops of rosemary, geranium, or lavender oil.

2 ▼ Put the top on the bottle, tighten, and shake it to mix the oils together.

3 Label the bottle with the name of your oil and what it does. Decorate the label using felt-tip pens and tie a colored ribbon around the lid.

YOUR SCENTED LAMP

If you want to fill a room with the aroma of your scented oils (see page 89), this lamp is easy to make. But remember, *always* ask an adult to light your lamp, and *never* touch it once it is lit.

(see page 89)

You will need

DAS clay, strong glue, a rolling pin, two empty yogurt cartons, a small blunt knife, paint, Vaseline, varnish, a small candle, rosemary, lavender, or geranium oil.

1 ▾ Split the clay into two balls, each measuring three inches around. Then roll out the balls into two flat circles, each measuring five inches across.

2 ▾ Cut one yogurt carton in half. Cover the outside of the bottom half with a coat of Vaseline.

3 ▾ Cover the outside of the other, whole, carton with Vaseline. Press one clay circle around the sides only. Trim off any extra clay.

5 Cut an arch out of the clay on the larger carton with your knife. Let both cartons dry.

4 ▸ Press the other clay circle over the sides and base of the half carton. Trim the edges with a blunt knife.

6 Remove the cartons. Paint the molds on the outsides only. When dry, put the larger mold on an old saucer. Rest the clay top, safely, on the base.

7 ▾ Put a few drops of one of your scented oils into the top with a tablespoon of water.

8 Place your lamp away from anything that might catch fire. Put a small candle in the base, and ask an adult to light it. The room will be filled with the sweet scent of your oil.

LIPSMACKIN' LATKES

One of the customs during Hanukkah is to eat fried food. The most traditional of all the fried foods are latkes—potato pancakes. Try these simple recipes for sweet and savory latkes!

You will need

3 medium sized potatoes
1 small onion
2 tablespoons flour
2 eggs (beaten)
1/2 teaspoon salt
vegetable oil for frying
a colander, a grater,
a strainer
paper towels
deep skillet

1 Ask an adult to preheat the oven to 200°F.

2 Peel and grate the potatoes into a colander, then leave to drain in the sink. Grate the onion and drain the juice through a strainer.

3 ▶ Mix the potatoes and onion together in a bowl. Stir in the flour, eggs, and salt. Now line a colander with paper towels.

4 ▶ Ask an adult to heat enough oil to fry in a deep skillet. When the oil sizzles, drop in tablespoons of the mixture—spaced apart. Flatten with the back of a spoon. Fry each side until golden brown.

5 ▶ Using a spatula, put the latkes in the lined colander so that the paper can soak up extra oil. Then transfer them to an ovenproof dish and into the oven to keep warm while you make the next batch!

6 ▶ Try switching one potato in the recipe with a small grated zucchini, beet, or carrot to make green, purple, or orange latkes!

BE SURE YOU DON'T BURN YOUR TONGUE!

SWEET CHEESE LATKES

Cheese is a traditional food at this time, so let's cook up some cheesy latkes . . . .

1 Beat the cheese, eggs, flour, butter, sugar, and vanilla flavoring together until smooth and creamy.

2 Lightly grease a large skillet with oil. Put in two tablespoons of the mixture. With an adult, fry the latkes on medium heat until both sides are golden brown. Serve with jelly, ice cream, or applesauce. . . .yummy!

You will need

1 cup of ricotta or cottage cheese
2 large eggs
2 tablespoons flour
1 stick butter
1 tablespoon sugar
1 teaspoon vanilla flavoring
vegetable oil for frying

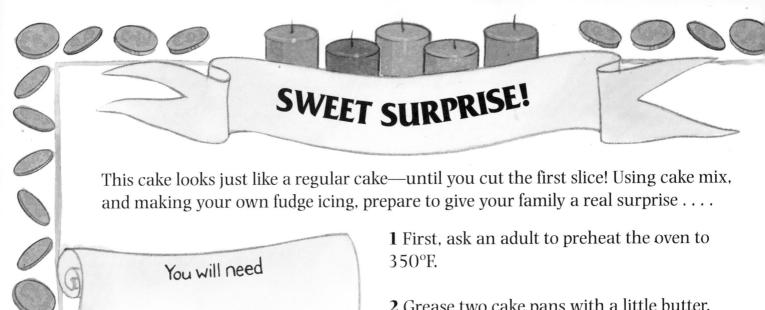

SWEET SURPRISE!

This cake looks just like a regular cake—until you cut the first slice! Using cake mix, and making your own fudge icing, prepare to give your family a real surprise . . . .

You will need

1 box cake mix
3½ cups of sugar
2 cups of milk
1 stick of butter, plus extra for greasing the pans
1 medium bar of plain chocolate
2 cake pans, M & Ms, chocolate coins

1 First, ask an adult to preheat the oven to 350°F.

2 Grease two cake pans with a little butter. Now make your cake mix, following the instructions on the box, and fill the pans.

To make your fudge icing . . .

3 Ask an adult to help you dissolve the sugar into the milk over medium heat. Bring to a boil, then simmer for two minutes.

4 With an adult, remove the pan from the heat and stir in the chocolate pieces and the butter. Stir over low heat until the chocolate melts. Pour it into a bowl and let it cool.

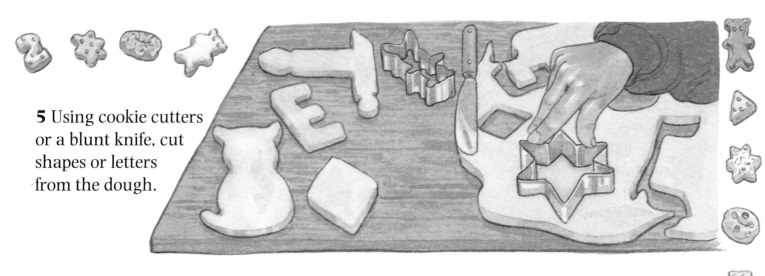

5 Using cookie cutters or a blunt knife, cut shapes or letters from the dough.

6 Prick the shapes with a fork. Put them on the cookie sheets, and ask an adult to place them in the oven for 12—15 minutes, then remove them. Leave to cool for five minutes, then put them on a wire rack to cool completely.

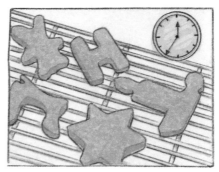

For instant iced treats, take your cookies, a box of plain doughnuts, a cup of sifted confectioners' sugar, colored sprinkles, and make some. . .

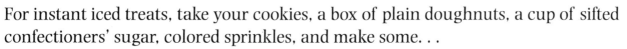

ENTICING ICING

Put the sugar into a bowl. Gradually add drops of hot water. Stir until the mixture is smooth and thick enough to coat the back of the spoon. Spread evenly onto your cookies and doughnuts, throw on colored sprinkles, leave to set. . .and serve!

YOUR HEBREW LETTERS

The Hebrew letters you have seen inside this book are *Nun, Gimel, Heh,* and *Shin,* and they have a special meaning at Hanukkah. The letters stand for the words *Nes gadol hayah sham,* which means "a great miracle happened there." In Israel they say *Nes gadol hayah po*— "a great miracle happened *here.*" The miracle is of the Hanukkah lights burning for eight days and nights. The letters shown here should always be read from right to left and should always go on the dreidel in the order shown below. . . .

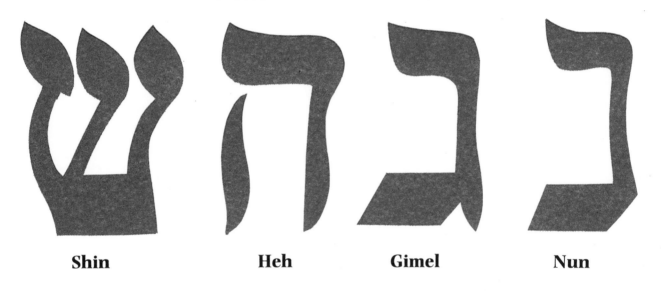

Shin   **Heh**   **Gimel**   **Nun**

Have fun making all the things inside this book, and have the happiest of Hanukkahs!

CHRISTMAS FUN

Holiday Treats

There are lots of different ways to count down to Christmas—one of the most fun is the Advent calendar, which has little doors to open on each of the days between December 1 and Christmas Eve.

Here's a holiday calendar with a difference—it has three sides, looks like a tree, and has a special treat in store every day. Why not make one as a surprise for your family and friends this Christmas?

You will need:

thin cardboard
24 tiny treats (candies, small toys, costume jewelry, pencil sharpeners, erasers)
cellophane tape
paints
needle and thread

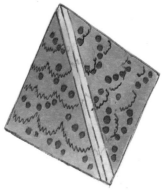

4. Tie or tape a tiny present to a piece of thread. Thread the other end with the needle, and push it through the tree from the inside.

2. Fold along the dotted lines to make a pyramid shape. Then tape the sides together, as shown.

1. Copy this pattern onto the cardboard, and cut it out. Paint the triangles to look like the sides of a Christmas tree.

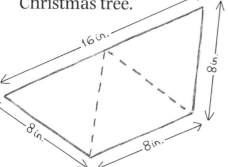

16 in.

8 in.

8 in.

8 in.

3. Draw 24 stars onto more cardboard, making them about 1 inch wide. Cut out the stars, paint them yellow or gold, and number them from 1 to 24.

5. Thread stars onto your tree. Pull the thread to hide the present inside the tree. Knot one end to hold it in place.

6. Do the same thing with the rest of the presents and stars, spreading them evenly over the tree.

7. Hang up the tree by threading a final piece of thread through the top, and knotting it on the inside.

On December 1, use scissors to snip off star number 1!

Welcome Wreath

Wreaths are traditional at Christmas and they're a good way of welcoming visitors at this time of the year. Look out for cones and greenery during a winter walk—or in your backyard!

You will need:

base for the wreath: ask an adult to help you make one (see step 1), or buy one from a florist • small fir or spruce branches and cones • holly or mistletoe green string • red ribbon thin wire

1. To make a base, ask an adult to help you twist some garden wire into a circle. Pack clumps of

moss around the wire, and tie them neatly in place with string or thin wire.

Little brothers and sisters can make this simple paper wreath. You'll need cardboard and some green and red paper (you could use colored paper from old magazines).

1. Draw a ring shape onto cardboard, and cut it out.

Attach evergreen sprigs to the base with string or thin wire. Overlap them to face all the same way. You could add cones, cranberries, or tangerines.

2. Tear or cut leaves from green paper, and glue around the ring so that they overlap. Cut berry and cone shapes from colored paper, and glue to the leaves.

Finish by tying a big red ribbon in a bow at the top.

3. Cut a seasonal shape from an old Christmas card. Hang from the middle with thread.

Christmas Cards

Why buy Christmas cards when they're much more fun to make at home?

Printed cards

You will need:

thin cardboard
Christmas cookie cutters
thin foam or sponge
thick cardboard
glue
poster paints

1. Fold several pieces of cardboard in half, and put them to one side.

2. Draw around one cutter onto thick card-board. Cut out the shape.

3. Lay the shape on the sponge, and draw around it. Cut out the sponge shape and glue to the cardboard to make a printing block.

4. Mix thick paint in a saucer. Dip the sponge in the paint and press onto the front of a folded card. Repeat to make many more cards.

5. You can also use your blocks to print matching patterns on envelopes, gift tags, and wrapping paper!

Santa's Reindeer

You will need:

thin cardboard—
about 10 x 8 inches
pencil
scissors
poster paints

1. Fold the cardboard in half, and copy the reindeer design. Make sure that the folded edge is at the top.

2. Cut out the reindeer, and cut along the line of its antlers. Press the head down slightly.

3. Paint the reindeer, or leave it white. You can write a message inside, or on the back.

Christmas Collage

You will need:

thin cardboard
scraps of fabric or paper, beads, etc.
scissors
glue

1. Fold the cardboard in half, and sketch a simple design on the front.

2. Cut or tear your scraps into shapes that fit your design. Then just glue them in position.

Trimming the Tree

People have been using evergreens to brighten up the home in wintertime for hundreds of years, but the idea of covering a tree with toys and baubles only began during the 1800s. Here are some special decorations to hang on the tree this year—they also make good presents after Christmas.

You will need:

thick yarn
scissors
scraps of fabric
needle and thread

Christmas Tree People

1. Wrap yarn ten times around your palm, and snip off the end (1). Tie one end (2), then tie again (3) to make the head and body.

2. Make another loop of yarn (4), and tie each end for the arms and hands.

3. Push the arms through the body, and attach by tying the joint with a piece of yarn.

4. Cut straight across the bottom of the doll. For a boy, tie the bottom into pants (5). For a girl, make a skirt from fabric scraps (6).

5. Cut eyes and mouths from tiny scraps of cloth, and glue on to make faces.

Cornucopias

You will need:

colored cardboard
red and green paper
scissors
glue
thin ribbon
colorful candies

1. Cut the cardboard into squares, each about 6 inches wide, and roll the cardboard into a cone shape.

2. Overlap the sides of the cone, and glue them together.

3. Cut green holly leaves and red berries from the colored paper, and glue them to the front.

4. Punch a hole near the top of the cornucopia, and thread it with ribbon. Fill with brightly-colored candies and hang on the tree.

Window Dressing

The glowing colors of these "stained glass" windows will warm up even the frostiest of Christmas mornings!

Add an indoor snowstorm made from cotton balls, and you'll soon have the best-dressed windows in town. . . .

Stained Glass

You will need:

two large sheets of black construction paper
colored tissue paper
thin chalk
scissors • glue

1. Pin or clip the pieces of black paper together.

2. Use chalk to draw this design on the top piece of paper. Cut the holes from both thicknesses of paper with scissors.

3. Cut out tissue paper shapes the same size as the window holes.

4. Glue the tissue pieces over all the holes in one piece of black paper.

5. Glue the other piece of black paper over the top, and then tape to your windowpane.

A Snowstorm

You will need:

white cotton balls
white or clear thread
needle

2. Thread some cotton balls onto each length, leaving a gap of 2-3 inches between each ball. Attach to the top of a window as shown.

1. Cut several lengths from the thread, each about 15 inches long. Thread the first piece onto a needle, and tie a knot at the end.

Nativity Scene

Here's a beautiful model Nativity scene for Christmas.
It's great fun to make, and a good way to remember
what happened on that very first Christmas Eve,
nearly 2,000 years ago. . . .

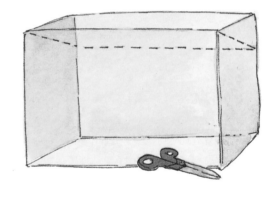

For the stable, you'll need:

a shoebox, or other small
cardboard box
a handful of thin twigs
scissors
glue

▶ Ask an adult to help you cut any flaps off the box.
Then lay the box on its side, and cut the top at an
angle, as shown in the picture.

◀ Cut holes in the two side
pieces, so that just a basic
frame is left. Then take your
twigs and brush off any dirt
or leaves.

▶ Snap the twigs to the length you need, and glue inside the back of the box. Then glue twigs over the side pieces of the frame.

▶ Measure between A and B on your box, and break several twigs to this length. Glue them side by side to make a roof, and glue onto the box when dry.

◀ To make the manger, just fold a small piece of cardboard in half, and glue two twigs in a crisscross at each end.

Making the Figures

To make the figures, you'll need to mix up some home-made salt dough. You'll also need some poster paints, and a little varnish to protect the figures.

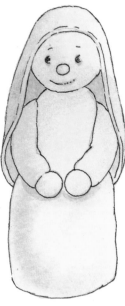

1. Roll a thick sausage from dough, for the body. Roll thin sausages for arms, with small balls for hands.

2. Roll a ball for the head, and a tiny blob for the nose. Press in a pencil to make the eyes and mouth.

3. Cut a thin square of dough to make the headdress. Drape over the head and body.

4. Add any extra features, then stand the figures on foil on a cookie sheet.

5. Let them dry out in a cool oven (250°F), for about three hours. Paint and varnish them when they've cooled down.

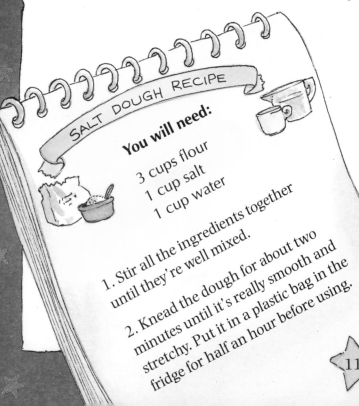

SALT DOUGH RECIPE

You will need:

3 cups flour
1 cup salt
1 cup water

1. Stir all the ingredients together until they're well mixed.

2. Knead the dough for about two minutes until it's really smooth and stretchy. Put it in a plastic bag in the fridge for half an hour before using.

▶ Make sheep from sausages and balls of dough. Roughen the backs with a fork before you bake them.

◀ Make angel hair by pushing dough through a garlic press. Glue on a halo and wings made from cardboard, and paint them gold.

The infant Jesus is made from a sausage and ball of dough. ▼

▼ Make a hole through one of the shepherds' hands with a toothpick before baking. Later, add a crook made from a pipe cleaner.

◀ This king has a crown and a beard made from dough (if the bits come off during baking, they can be glued on again before painting). The box is made from a cube of dough.

The Butcher, the Baker...

In France, children have some unusual-looking characters in their Nativity scenes. As well as the Nativity figures, you'll often see ordinary townspeople, such as the mayor and the butcher!

Dangly Santa

You can trace the shapes on these pages to make a little decoration or copy them at a much bigger size. How about making a really huge Santa to hang up in the hall?

You will need:

red, white, and black cardboard
scissors • glue
cotton balls
needle and thread

1. Trace or copy the boots onto black cardboard, and the eyes onto white cardboard. Copy the rest onto red cardboard, and cut all the pieces out.

2. Cut black and white cardboard to make the hands, belt, and buckle, and glue to both sides of the body.

3. Glue cotton balls to make the trim for the coat, boots, and hat, and for the eyebrows and mustache. Decorate both sides of the pieces.

4. Use short lengths of thread to link all the parts of the Santa together, and hang from the ceiling.

Christmas Cookbook

The kitchen is often busy at Christmas, but you may be able to persuade the Chief Cook to let you make these special treats! *Always* ask an adult to help when you're cooking.

Christmas Pizza

You will need:

ready-made pizza dough (grapefruit size)
1/3 cup pizza sauce
1 green pepper
cheese slices
stuffed olives
a few anchovies • flour

Great fun for lunch, or as part of a buffet if you have guests coming over. . .

Before you begin, set the oven to 425°F.

1. On a lightly floured surface, roll out the dough into a circle. Grease a pizza pan and press in the dough until it fits.

2. Spread the pizza sauce over the dough.

3. Cut green pepper into thin slices, and arrange to look like a Christmas tree.

4. Cut strips of cheese for the candles, and halve the olives for the flames. Make the trunk from anchovies.

5. Ask an adult to put the pizza in the oven, and bake for 25 minutes. The dough should be crisp and golden brown.

Christmas Cookies

Use cookie cutters to make Christmas shapes to hang on the tree, or cut out giant shapes with a blunt knife....

You will need:

1/3 cup butter
1 egg
1 1/2 cups flour
2 oz. corn syrup
1/2 cup light brown sugar
1 tsp. cinnamon
1 tsp. ginger

Set the oven to 350°F.

1. Sift the flour, spices, and baking powder into a big bowl. Add the sugar, and rub in the butter to make fine breadcrumbs.

4. Lay the shapes on a greased cookie sheet, and ask an adult to cook them for about 15 minutes.

3. Roll out the dough to about 1/4 inch thick. Cut Christmas shapes from the dough and, using a toothpick, make holes in the tops.

2. Beat the egg and syrup together, and add to the flour—mix into a dough. Place in a freezer bag and refrigerate for half an hour.

5. Decorate them when they're cool—use confectioners' sugar, 1 tbsp. water, and a little food coloring. Thread ribbon through the holes.

Perfect Presents

Make your favorite grown-ups happy this Christmas by giving them homemade presents! The ideas on these pages are so quick and easy that you may even consider going into mass production. . . .

Print-a-T-shirt

You will need:

plain white cotton T-shirt to fit your grown-up
fabric paints or pens (pens for outlines, paints for big areas of color)
paper • cardboard

1. Sketch out some designs for your T-shirt on the paper.

2. Push cardboard inside the T-shirt and pin it flat. Paint your design onto the front, and leave it to dry.

NOTE: Many fabric paints need to be ironed to make them colorfast. If so, ask an adult to help.

SECOND NOTE: It's just as easy to paint an apron, a pair of shorts, or a pillowcase!

Fridge Magnets

You will need:

self-hardening clay
Christmas cookie
cutters
poster paints
waterproof varnish
small magnets • glue

1. Roll out the clay until it's about 1 inch thick.

2. Cut out shapes with the cookie cutters, and leave them in a warm place to dry out completely. For small objects this will take about 24 hours.

3. Paint and varnish the shapes. When they're dry, glue a magnet to the back of each one.

Santa Bath Mitten

You will need:

your hand
thin foam or terry cloth
(red, white, and black,
if possible)
a needle and thread
a felt-tipped
pen

1. Use your hands as guides for drawing two mitten shapes on the foam, allowing an extra 1/2 inch all round. Cut the mitten shapes out.

2. Sew together, leaving the bottom open, and turn inside out. Cut the hat, trim, and features from extra foam, and sew to the mitten.

Christmas Wildlife

It's great being outdoors on a frosty morning—unless you happen to be a bird. It's hard for them to find food and water when the ground is frozen, and many go hungry. By giving them their own Christmas tree, you could help to save their lives.

► Choose a tree in your backyard to decorate. If you only have a small yard, tie big sticks together, and "plant" them in a big pot.

▼ Spread pinecones with peanut butter, roll them in birdseed, and hang on the tree with thread.

▲ Make garlands for the tree: thread a darning needle, and knot one end. Thread on peanuts in their shells, cranberries, or millet.

◀ Chunks of coconut or corn can be hung up with ribbon, or try making holes in apples, and studding them with seeds.

▶ Don't forget water! Put some out in a shallow bowl, but well away from cats.

Spare a thought for all the trees that are felled each Christmas. You don't have to buy a cut tree—why not choose a living one, which will go on growing for years and years? Most pines and firs can be kept in pots. When they start to outgrow them, they can be planted outside.

After Christmas

Christmas doesn't have to end on December 26. Here are some things to do even after the day is over.

Discover how to be Very, Very Popular

. . . with the grown-ups, that is. Help with the household chores—and don't wait to be asked! (Remember, it's their holiday too. . .)

Christmas Collage

Make Christmas last longer by making a special collage. Use bits of wrapping paper, your favorite cards, snapshots, gift tags, party hats, tinsel, candy wrappers, party invitations —unless it moves, collage it! Glue to a piece of cardboard, or stick in a scrapbook.

Get in Touch

With a bit of thought and imagination, sending thank-you letters need never be boring. If you can't think of anything interesting to say, you could print some good-looking cards and envelopes (see page 102), and just add a short thank-you message.

New Year Promises

If you can't think of any New Year's resolutions, maybe your friends, brothers, and sisters will have some suggestions. . . Make a list of resolutions and pin them to the wall. Give yourself 10 points each week in the New Year that you keep them. Can you make it to 100?

KWANZAA FUN

The History of Kwanzaa

Kwanzaa is a holiday that celebrates the African tradition of gathering together at the end of the harvest. It was created in 1966 by Dr. Maulana Karenga, a professor and cultural leader. He wanted to help African Americans to remember their heritage. He also hoped Kwanzaa would be an annual reminder of the importance of sharing with family and friends, and that this would help build a sense of African-American community throughout the United States.

Kwanzaa begins on December 26 and lasts until January 1. There is a principle for each day of Kwanzaa. These seven principles help us to think about our lives and future, and promote a sense of pride in African-American culture.

The word kwanzaa comes from the African trade language Swahili. In Swahili, *kwanza* is a word from a phrase which means "first fruits." Dr. Karenga added an extra "a" to remind us that it is different from the original word.

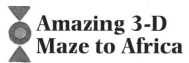

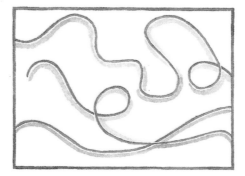
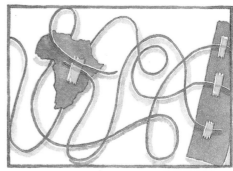

The Seven Days of Kwanzaa

December 26
Unity

Umoja
(oo-MOE-jah)

December 27
Self Determination

Kujichagulia
(koo-jee-cha-goo-LEE-ah)

December 28
Collective Work & Responsibility

Ujima
(oo-JEE-mah)

Use the seven principles to improve yourself and to help others.

December 29
Cooperative Economics

Ujamaa
(oo-JAH-mah)

December 30
Purpose

Nia
(nee-AH)

December 31
Creativity

Kuumba
(koo-OOM-bah)

January 1
Faith

Imani
(ee-MAH-nee)

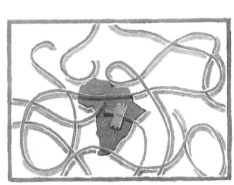

3. The adult should then mix up all of the yarn, creating a large, loose tangle—but not too tangled!

4. Remove each piece of yarn from the paper and give one end to each player. Untangle the maze to find who gets to Africa!

Kwanzaa symbols

To celebrate Kwanzaa with your family, put the seven symbols of Kwanzaa on a low table each night during the holiday. Kwanzaa symbols help teach and strengthen the basic principles of Kwanzaa. The kikombe (*kee-COAM-bay*) is the cup that symbolizes unity. It is used only in the libation ceremony (see page 144). Here are the other symbols of Kwanzaa.

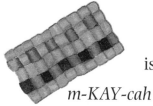

m-KAY-cah

Mkeka
is a straw mat. It reminds us of our African traditions.

Vibunzi
are ears of corn. They remind us of the importance of children.

vi-BUN-zee

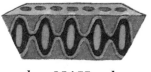

kee-NAH-rah

Kinara
is a seven-branch candle holder. It says that we all came from the same place.

Mazao
are the fruits and vegetables of the harvest. They remind us of the rewards of working together.

mah-ZAH-oh

sah-WAH-dee

Mishumaa Saba
are the seven candles that remind us of the principles of Kwanzaa. We light one each day, beginning with the black one in the middle.

mee-SHOO-maah sah-BAH

6 4 2 1 3 5 7

Zawadi
are the gifts. Handmade gifts are given at Kwanzaa for work well done and to encourage children to practice the seven principles all year long, not just during Kwanzaa.

Kinara and Mishuma Saba

You will need
red, green, and black construction paper (8½" x 11")
• scissors • glue • double-sided tape • paint or glitter

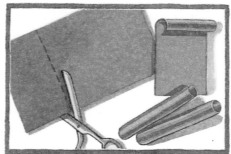

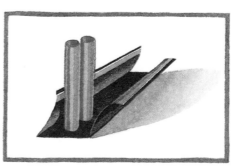

1. Fold one piece of the paper into thirds the long way. Decorate the outside. Place double-sided tape along the long edges of the paper on the inside only.

2. For candles, cut sheets of construction paper in half the short way. Roll three pieces each of red and green paper, and one of black, into tubes. Secure them with tape.

3. Stand the candle holder upright. Bring one end of the paper up and stick the candles in position. Bring the other end of the paper up and press the edges together.

4. To make the candle flames, cut out flame shapes and color them yellow or add glitter. Tape a flame to the inside of the black candle on the first day of Kwanzaa. "Light" the red candle next to it on the second day, then the green, and so on.

Special phrases

There are some important phrases used in the Kwanzaa celebration. These phrases are in the African language of Swahili. You can learn these basic Swahili words by sounding them out. You can practice speaking the Swahili words that are part of the Kwanzaa celebration with your family and friends.

Habari Gani (*ha-BAH-ree GAH-nee*)
During Kwanzaa we greet each other by saying "Habari Gani," which means "What's new?" Answer by saying the name of the principle being celebrated that day. On the first day of Kwanzaa when someone says "Habari Gani," you answer by saying "Umoja." On day five of Kwanzaa, when someone says "Habari Gani," your answer should be "Nia."

Harambee (*hah-ROM-beh*)
The harambee means "Let's pull together." It is the Kwanzaa call for unity. The harambee is performed in sets of seven to honor the seven principles. The harambee should be done after the libation ceremony and at the end of the celebration, but it can also be done on any occasion when you want to strengthen the spirit of unity.

Family Tree

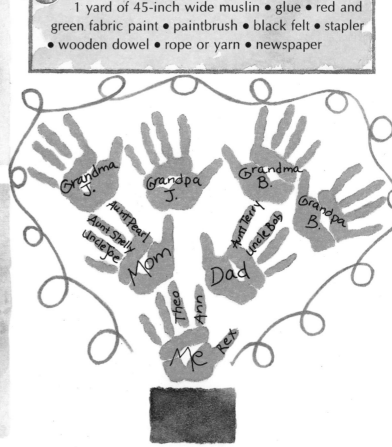

You will need
1 yard of 45-inch wide muslin • glue • red and green fabric paint • paintbrush • black felt • stapler • wooden dowel • rope or yarn • newspaper

Welcome Banner

You will need
5 pieces of felt 8½ x 11 inches • at least
3 yards of 1-inch wide ribbon • scissors
• acrylic writing paint (or glitter and glue)
• double-sided tape or glue

Fold each piece of felt in half the long way and cut into two pieces. Then fold each piece in half again (but do not cut!) to make ten folded pieces.

Paint one letter of the word "HABARI GANI" on the front of each piece of felt and let dry. Spread the ribbon out and tape or glue each piece of felt to the ribbon in its fold. Make sure you space each letter equally.

1. Put down newspaper to protect your work surface. Cut a tree trunk shape slightly larger than your hand from the black felt. Glue securely at the center bottom of the muslin. Squirt red fabric paint on your hands and smooth it over your palms.

2. Carefully place your palm down above the middle of the top of the tree trunk. Above your handprint, make two prints for your parents. Finally, make four more on top for your grandparents. Then go back and write in all the names of your relatives.

3. Finish your family tree by painting a green loop of leaves around the handprints. To hang it up, fold the top of the muslin over two inches and staple closed, as shown. Slide in the dowel and tie yarn to each end. Display your heritage proudly!

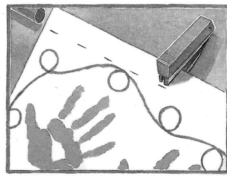

The Nguzo Saba (EN-goo-zoh-SAH-bah)

That's Swahili for "seven principles." The seven principles are a very important part of Kwanzaa. Each principle is a value or a goal that we should practice and live by all year long. There is one principle for each day of Kwanzaa.

UMOJA ★ Unity

The first day of Kwanzaa emphasizes the need to work for and keep unity in your family, among your friends, and in your neighborhood. We strive for peace everywhere by living in harmony, and playing and working together.

Unity Dolls

You will need
brown construction paper • yarn • fabric scraps • scissors

1. Fold the construction paper in half and then in half again. Draw and cut out a doll figure. Be careful not to cut across the hands.

2. Open it up and you will have four dolls connected at the hands. Paste yarn and scrap pieces of fabric to each doll for hair and clothes.

Unity dolls need to hold hands in order to stand up. Use tape to connect the dolls on each end at the hands.

Afrocentric Vest

You will need
large brown paper bag • scissors • fabric scraps or markers

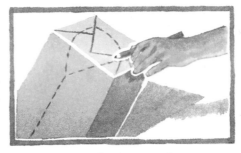

1. Open up the paper bag and mark it as shown. Cut along the lines, cutting out front and neck openings. Also make two cuts across the bottom sides of the bag.

2. Have an adult press the bag flat with an iron on low heat. Draw lines for the arm holes, as shown. Make sure they are big enough for you and then cut them out.

3. Decorate in traditional African patterns by gluing on scraps of fabric, or draw your designs with markers or crayons.

KUJICHAGULIA ★ Self Determination

The second day of Kwanzaa concentrates on deciding for yourself, believing in yourself, and taking responsibility for your own decisions and actions.

Look through old magazines and cut out pictures you like. It is fun to stick to a theme, like family or African-American history.

Jigsaw Puzzle

You will need
old magazines • scissors • glue • empty cereal box

1. Cut out the front of the box to use as a base. Cut out your pictures from old magazines and place them overlapping each other on the cardboard.

2. Once you have covered all the space on the cardboard and have the pictures the way you want, paste them in position. Make sure each picture is glued down completely. Let dry.

3. Draw wiggly jigsaw lines on the back of the puzzle. Cut out the shapes. Have your friends put the puzzle back together. Can they guess the theme?

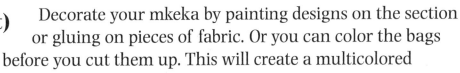

Mkeka (African Mat)

You will need
2-3 grocery bags
• tape • fabric scraps
• paint or coloring pens
• ruler • scissors • pencil

Decorate your mkeka by painting designs on the section or gluing on pieces of fabric. Or you can color the bags before you cut them up. This will create a multicolored design when you weave.

1. Pull apart the seam in the back and at the bottom of the bag. Flatten the bag and cut it the long way into strips three inches wide.

2. Lay 8 strips together on a flat surface, set the remaining strips aside. Use tape to hold down one side of the strips, leaving at least 2 inches at the ends. Now you are ready to weave.

3. Take one of the remaining strips and go over and under the flat strips. The next strip should go under and over in the opposite sequence. The strip after that should go over and under again.

4. Leave about 2 inches unwoven on the bottom and around the sides. Then fold all the ends under and tape them securely, carefully working your way around each edge of your mkeka.

UJIMA ★ Collective Work and Responsibility

Day 3

The third day of Kwanzaa focuses on working together. We work together to help others and to build a better community. We also work together to find solutions to problems and to overcome hardship.

🔘 African Mask

You will need
a balloon • newspapers • 2 cups flour • 4 cups warm water • ½ cup white glue • paints (various colors) • scissors

1. Mix the flour, water, and glue into a paste. Tear up old newspapers into strips. Dip the strips into the paste.

2. Cover the balloon with a layer of strips. Let dry thoroughly. Pop the balloon. Cut in half the long way.

3. Attach cardboard ears with tape. Cut out eyes. Cover the entire mask with several layers of newspaper.

4. When the mask is dry, paint it. You can also decorate your mask with things like beads or yarn.

Traditionally, Africans wore masks to feel brave in battle and when hunting. Today, masks are also worn for celebrations such as birth, marriage, or harvest.

Nguzo Saba Mobile

You will need
paper plate • cardboard • hole punch • stapler • paint • yarn • scissors

1. Draw a spiral on the paper plate as shown. Carefully cut along this line. Cut out seven squares of cardboard (one for each principle) to hang from the mobile.

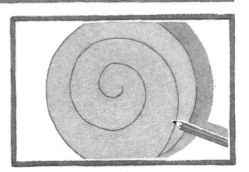

2. Pierce a hole at the top of each square with the hole punch. Pierce holes through the paper plate, with one through the middle. Tie a piece of yarn to each square and thread the other end through a hole in the plate. Secure with a large knot.

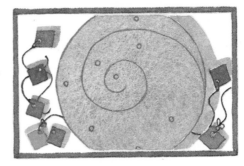

3. Decorate the squares and the paper plate with the seven principles. Tie one more piece of yarn through the hole in the middle of the paper plate. Your mobile is ready to hang!

You can make many other types of mobile too. Try a safari mobile with African animals, or a family mobile with pictures of the members of your family, or a friend mobile.

UJAMAA ★ Cooperative Economics

The fourth day of Kwanzaa is about using our money and talents wisely so that we all may prosper. We cooperate by sharing money, taking responsibility for our work, buying things together, and using our money to help others who are in need.

Savings Bank

You will need
4 toilet-paper tubes • colored paper • plastic wrap • tape scissors • glue • small block of wood

1. This bank will hold pennies, nickels, dimes, and quarters. Use scissors to cut a strip out of each of the four tubes, as shown.

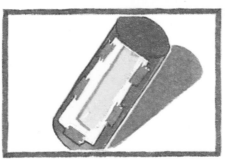

2. Cover each hole with a piece of plastic wrap. Tape it in place. This will be the window through which you can watch your savings grow.

3. Decorate the outside of each tube with a mosaic of paper. Let dry. Glue the tubes onto a wooden block or piece of heavy cardboard.

African Trade Beads

You will need
DAS or other oven bake clay (in several colors) • glue • round toothpicks • knife • rolling pin • wax paper

African trade beads are beautiful multicolored beads that were used to trade with African merchants in the 1800s. You can make your own.

Rub cold clay between your hands to soften. Square or round beads made from one color of clay are the easiest to make.

For more complicated beads, roll some clay flat between two sheets of wax paper with a rolling pin to make a sheet of clay. Remove wax paper and cut out shapes with a butter knife. Stick them together to make just about anything!

To make multicolored beads, roll different colors of long round logs together. Place several logs together and slice to reveal a pattern. Take tiny bits of different colors and stick them together to form swirly beads.

Use toothpicks to make holes in the beads. Follow the instructions on the package for baking. String beads together to make necklaces or bracelets. To connect, attach clasps or tie a large bead to one end and make a loop in the other.

Nia ★ Purpose

Day 5

The fifth day of Kwanzaa reminds us to have a plan for the future and to use our talents and abilities to achieve that purpose. When we can, we should also help others to develop their talents and achieve their goals.

Book Holder

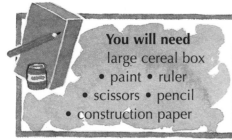

You will need
large cereal box
• paint • ruler
• scissors • pencil
• construction paper

This holder can be used to store books that are related to your purpose or can help you achieve it.

1. Make sure your cereal box is large enough to hold your books or magazines. Carefully cut off the top part of the box as shown.

2. Decorate by covering with a collage of colored paper. You could also decorate with leftover wallpaper or your favorite stickers.

Nia Scroll

NIA — My purpose is to be positive.

You will need
scrap of fabric • red or green construction paper
• scissors • glue • 12 inches of ribbon • marker

Tie your scroll with ribbon and put it in a secret place. Read it next Kwanzaa— see if your purpose has changed.

1. You can make 4 scrolls with one piece of paper. Cut the construction paper into 4 strips the long way. Use one strip of paper as a pattern to cut out a strip of fabric.

⏳ ○ Terrarium

You will need
large jar • pebbles • charcoal • potting soil, small plants (ferns, ivy, moss) • rocks • sticks

Put ¹/₂ inch of pebbles in the bottom of the jar, then put ¹/₂ inch of charcoal on top of the pebbles. Next put about 4 inches of potting soil on top of the charcoal. Place the plants in an attractive arrangement in the jar. Add a little water to make the soil damp. Add a few sticks and rocks to make it scenic. Screw on the lid of the jar and have an adult poke a few holes in the lid. Add a few drops of water each week. Place the jar in a sunny place and watch your plants grow.

2. Spread glue on one side of the paper. Glue the cloth to the paper so it fits exactly. Let it dry. Write the word "NIA" on the left side of the paper and write your purpose on the right side.

KUUMBA ★ Creativity

Day 6

The sixth day of Kwanzaa is about expressing yourself creatively through music, art, dance, and thought. Kuumba is also about beautifying your living environment, such as your home or neighborhood.

Tambourine

You will need
2 aluminum pie pans • ribbons (red, green, and black) • hole punch • 4 small bells • stapler • scissors

Horn

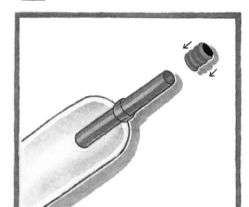

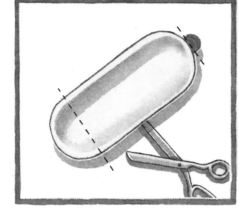

1. Ask an adult to cut off the bottom of a plastic bottle and to cut off the top part of a second plastic bottle to make a mouthpiece.

2. Roll some thin cardboard up to fit inside the plastic bottle. Take the "mouthpiece" and fit it on top of the tube. Secure everything with tape.

1. Place the brims of the two pie pans together and staple them in four places. Use the hole punch to make four holes in the brim of the pie pan.

2. Cut four pieces of ribbon 12 inches long. Thread each ribbon through a bell and tie it through one of the holes. Decorate by stapling extra ribbons around the brim.

Scrapper

Cut two pieces of sandpaper and glue them to two small blocks of wood. Rub together for an interesting sound.

African Rain Stick

You will need
long cardboard tube (empty gift wrap roll) • piece of flat cardboard • scissors • masking tape • pen • 2½ cups of split peas • paint • yarn

1. Use the bottom of the tube to trace seven circles on the flat cardboard. Cut out the circles. Cut five circles in half, leaving the other two whole.

2. Fold the tube in half the long way and cut a straight line from one end to the other on both sides. Place the two half tubes next to each other.

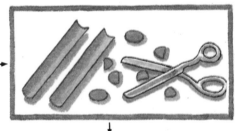

4. Pour the peas into the tube. Close with the last cardboard circle and tape. Wrap masking tape around the entire tube. Decorate. Turn the stick upside down and listen to the "rain."

3. Securely tape five half circles to the inside of each tube. Make sure that the half circles do not touch each other and tape the tube back together again. Tape one end closed with a cardboard circle.

Imani ★ Faith

The seventh day of Kwanzaa teaches us to believe with all our heart in our people, our parents, our teachers, and our leaders. We also believe in ourselves and our ability to succeed—as individuals and as a people.

Kwanzaa Memory Book

You will need
large sheet of construction paper • pencil • scissors • cardboard • glue • paints

1. Cut the construction paper into three strips the long way. This will be enough to make three books, so you could make Kwanzaa memory books to give as gifts for your family and friends.

2. Fold one strip in half. Then fold it in half twice more to make 8 panels. Cut two squares from the cardboard, each the size of one panel. Glue the squares to the outside panels.

3. Paint and decorate the cover of your book. Record the events of each day of Kwanzaa as they happen.

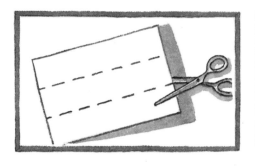

Blindfold Adventure ⚬ Treasure box

You will need
blindfolds for half
of the players

You will need
shoe box or gift box
• glue • fabric scraps
• beads • buttons • ribbon
• string • beans

This is a good
game to play at
Kwanzaa or
during family
get-togethers.

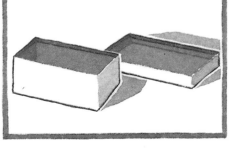

1. Line the inside of the box
with a large scrap of fabric,
gluing it securely around the
top edges. Use ribbon to line
the inside borders.

2. Paint the outside and
decorate it with ribbon, yarn,
feathers, buttons. Keep your
Kwanzaa treasures safely
inside.

Divide the players into teams of two. The
partner who goes first puts on the blindfold.
The other partner is the protector. It is the
protector's duty to take the blindfolded
partner around the room or house and to
protect them from any danger. See what
happens when you trust and cooperate
with your partner. See what happens when
you don't. Get ready, get set, go! Reverse
roles for the next adventure.

Kwanzaa Karamu

The Kwanzaa karamu is a lavish feast and cultural program that takes place on December 31. All are welcomed, and everyone brings a dish to share. The room is decorated in red, black, and green, and the seven Kwanzaa symbols are displayed prominently.

Program

Create a program for your Karamu celebration. Hand it out to your guests as they arrive.

Napkin Rings

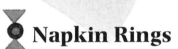

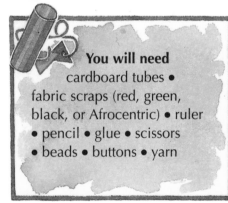

You will need
cardboard tubes • fabric scraps (red, green, black, or Afrocentric) • ruler • pencil • glue • scissors • beads • buttons • yarn

1. Measure 1 or 2 inches along the length of the cardboard tube. Cut out as many rings as you need.

2. Glue strips of fabric to the rings and decorate with yarn, beads, or paper. Add napkins and prepare to feast!

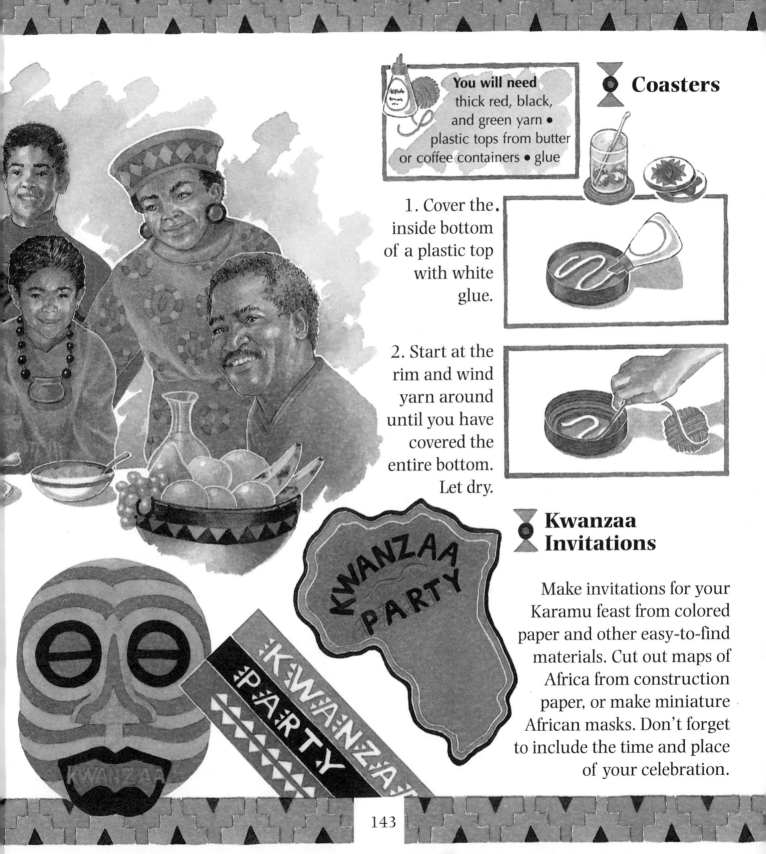

Coasters

You will need
thick red, black, and green yarn • plastic tops from butter or coffee containers • glue

1. Cover the inside bottom of a plastic top with white glue.

2. Start at the rim and wind yarn around until you have covered the entire bottom. Let dry.

Kwanzaa Invitations

Make invitations for your Karamu feast from colored paper and other easy-to-find materials. Cut out maps of Africa from construction paper, or make miniature African masks. Don't forget to include the time and place of your celebration.

KWANZAA PARTY

KWANZAA PARTY

KWANZAA

The Libation Ceremony

The Kwanzaa libation ceremony is very important. It begins with an older and respected friend or member of the family giving a toast. The toast is made to honor and praise our ancestors. Then the libation (water or juice) is sprinkled from the unity cup (a special cup that is only used for this purpose) onto the floor in the four directions: east, west, north, and south. The libation reminds us of the presence of the ancestors, and offering them a drink to quench their thirst keeps them alive in our memory. After giving the ancestors a drink, the unity cup is passed around and each member of the family takes a sip.

Libation Toasts

1. To our ancestors: let us honor and praise them and keep our memories of them alive
2. To the future
3. To children, our hope for the future
4. To building a strong community
5. To education, our children's key to the future

Unity Cup

The cup used for the libation ceremony is called the unity cup, or kikombe (*kee-COAM-bay*) in Swahili. You can make your own cup for this special occasion.

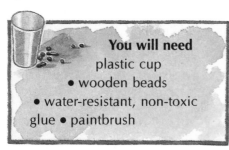

You will need
plastic cup
• wooden beads
• water-resistant, non-toxic glue • paintbrush

1. Brush a generous amount of glue around the outside of the cup. Leave about $3/4$ inch unglued around the rim. Let the glue dry until it is slightly tacky.

2. Press beads onto the cup to make a beautiful African design. Leave space around the rim so you can drink from it safely. Let it dry thoroughly.